An Introduction to Social Constructionism

An Introduction to Social Constructionism is a readable and critical account of social constructionism for students new to the field.

Focussing on the challenge to psychology that social constructionism poses, Vivien Burr examines the notion of 'personality' to illustrate the rejection of essentialism by social constructionists. This questions psychology's traditional understanding of the person. She then shows how the study of language can be used as a focus for our understanding of human behaviour and experience. This is continued by examining 'discourses' and their role in constructing social phenomena, and the relationship between discourse and power. However, the problems associated with these analyses are also clearly outlined.

Many people believe that one of the aims of social science should be to bring about social change. Vivien Burr analyses what possibilities there might be for change in social constructionist accounts. She also addresses what social constructionism means in practice to research in the social sciences, and includes some guidelines on doing discourse analysis.

An Introduction to Social Constructionism is an invaluable and clear guide for all perplexed students who want to begin to understand this difficult area.

Vivien Burr is a senior lecturer in psychology at the University of Huddersfield.

An Introduction to Social Constructionism

Vivien Burr

First published 1995
by Routledge
11 New Fetter Lane, London EC4P 4EE

Simultaneously published in the USA and Canada
by Routledge
29 West 35th Street, New York, NY 10001

Reprinted 1996, 1997, 1998 (twice), 1999 and 2000

Reprinted 2001 by Routledge
27 Church Road, Hove, East Sussex, BN3 2FA
29 West 35th Street, New York, NY 10001

Routledge is an imprint of the Taylor & Francis Group

Typeset in Palatino by
Florencetype Ltd, Stoodleigh, Devon
Printed and bound in the UK by TJ International Ltd, Padstow

British Library Cataloguing in Publication Data
A catalogue record for this book is available from the British Library

Library of Congress Cataloging in Publication Data
A catalogue record for this book has been requested

ISBN 0–415–10404–1 (hbk)
ISBN 0–415–10405–X (pbk)

Contents

Preface

This book is for students. As a lecturer teaching social psychology to Behavioural Sciences undergraduates, I have in recent years attempted to include in my teaching something of what I shall call the social constructionist movement within social psychology. This has proved to be a difficult task, partly because of the inherent difficulty of the subject matter, but also because of the dearth of reading material appropriate to the needs of students coming to social constructionist ideas for the first time. Although there exist a number of excellent books written from a social constructionist perspective (e.g. Potter and Wetherell, 1987; Weedon, 1987; Shotter, 1993a, 1993b; Parker, 1992), for the most part these appear to be written by academics for other academics. This book, then, is an attempt to redress the balance. Its primary aim is to introduce social constructionist ideas to social sciences students so that they may then be in a position to read and understand more advanced material. To this end, I have tried to explain the key concepts and terms clearly and simply, and have used illustrative examples as much as possible in order to help students gain a foothold in what may be to them quite alien territory. To guide students in their choice of more advanced reading, I have provided a short, annotated reading list at the end of each chapter. Sometimes it was an arbitrary decision whether to recommend a book or journal article in an earlier or a later chapter, and sometimes I have done both.

I believe that it is not possible to write about something in a completely impartial and dispassionate way, that is, taking up no personal stance at all with respect to the subject matter (and as it happens this itself appears to be consistent with a social constructionist view). One must (even if only to engage the interest of one's readers) decide whether one is on the whole an advocate or a critic of the material one is writing about. In writing this book, I have generally adopted the position of the advocate, so that my overall strategy has been to persuade the reader of the advantages of a social constructionist approach. However, this is not an uncritical advocacy, and a second major aim of this book is to point out the weaknesses, inadequacies and dangers of social constructionism and to indicate the areas where I believe there is still much to be resolved. As one who has as yet no history of publication or research in this area, I feel myself to be particularly free of axes to grind and reputations to defend, and therefore able to advocate and criticise with relative impugnity.

As an introductory text, some may feel that my account of social constructionism is somewhat idiosyncratic. However, while it may not be the story that another person would have told, I justify it on the grounds, firstly, that it concerns itself with social constructionist viewpoints that I believe students are likely to meet up with in their excursions into the literature, and, secondly, that it reflects the questions (built into the chapter titles) most commonly raised by students. Although the book is British in its emphasis, drawing examples from issues and everyday life in the UK and highlighting the debates current in British social constructionist writing, it brings together both British and North American contributions under a common umbrella. With respect to the illustrative examples that I use, I have endeavoured to render them meaningful to the North American reader.

Social constructionism is in a state of flux. It is a field of enquiry which is changing and expanding very rapidly, and it is therefore quite difficult to gain a stable perspective on the issues. This book is a 'snapshot' of what the social constructionist world looks like to me at present, and, like any snapshot, it is a likeness that is recognisable without passing itself off as the only true image. I hope that you find it useful.

Acknowledgements

I am indebted to all those who have suffered during the birth of this book. In particular, special recognition is due to Trevor Butt, who tirelessly read and commented upon earlier drafts, and to my great friend, Katrine Ellerd-Styles, who helped me to elaborate my ideas during many telephone conversations and still managed to remain full of enthusiasm and support. My thanks are also due to Dallas Cliff for readily providing me with some of his own material, and for his commitment to this project. And, bringing up the rear in this motley troupe, I must include my musical friend Geoff Adams for once again giving up his free time to prepare both indexes.

June 1994

Introduction

What is social constructionism?

Over the last fifteen years or so, students of the social sciences in Britain and North America have witnessed the gradual emergence of a number of alternative approaches to the study of human beings as social animals. These approaches have appeared under a variety of rubrics, such as 'critical psychology', 'discourse analysis', 'deconstruction' and 'poststructuralism'. What many of these approaches have in common, however, is what is now often referred to as 'social constructionism'. Social constructionism can be thought of as a theoretical orientation which to a greater or lesser degree underpins all of these newer approaches, which are currently offering radical and critical alternatives in psychology and social psychology, as well as in other disciplines in the social sciences and humanities. Social constructionism, as it has been taken up by psychology and social psychology, is the focus of this book, and my aim is to introduce the reader to some of its major features, while also elaborating upon the implications it holds for how we are to understand human beings, and for the discipline of psychology itself.

In this introductory chapter, my first task will be to say what kinds of writing and research I include within the term 'social constructionism', and why. This will not necessarily be where others would draw the boundary, but it will serve as an initial orientation for the reader, giving some indication of what it means to take a social constructionist approach. I will say something about the contributors to the field, and why I have included them as social constructionists. It is quite possible that I will be guilty of labelling as 'social constructionist' writers who would not wish to be labelled as such, and vice versa. I apologise in advance to those who feel uncomfortable with my description of them, but must adopt the rationale which appears to me to make sense of the area. I shall use the term 'social constructionism', rather than 'constructivism', throughout. These terms are sometimes used interchangeably, but Gergen (1985) recommends the use of 'constructionism', since 'constructivism' is sometimes used to refer to Piagetian theory and to a particular kind of perceptual theory, and could cause confusion.

I will then go on to outline something of the history of the social constructionist movement, especially as it has been taken up by social psychology. As we shall see, social constructionism as an approach to the social sciences draws its influences from a number of disciplines, including philosophy, sociology and linguistics, making it multidisciplinary in nature.

Finally, I shall raise the major issues that will be addressed by this book, indicating the chapters where they will be dealt with.

IS THERE A DEFINITION OF SOCIAL CONSTRUCTIONISM?

There is no single description which would be adequate for all the different kinds of writer whom I shall refer to as social constructionist. This is because, although different writers may share some characteristics with others, there is not really anything that they *all* have in common. What links them all together is a kind of 'family resemblance' (this is what Rosch (1973) meant by 'prototypes' or 'fuzzy sets'). Members of the same family differ in the family characteristics that they share. Mother and daughter may have the typical 'Smith nose', while father and son may have inherited from grandma Smith, who also has the Smith nose, their prominent ears. Cousin George may share the prominent ears, and also, like his aunt Harriet, have the Smith thick, curly hair. There is no one characteristic borne by all members of the Smith family, but there are enough recurrent features shared amongst different family members to identify the people as basically belonging to the same family group. This is the model I shall adopt for social constructionism. There is no one feature which could be said to identify a social constructionist position. Instead, we might loosely group as social constructionist any approach which has at its foundation one or more of the following key assumptions (from Gergen, 1985). You might think of these as something like 'things you would absolutely have to believe in order to be a social constructionist':

1 A critical stance towards taken-for-granted knowledge:

Social constructionism insists that we take a critical stance towards our taken-for-granted ways of understanding the world (including ourselves). It invites us to be critical of the idea that our observations of the world unproblematically yield its nature to us, to challenge the view that conventional knowledge is based upon objective, unbiased observation of the world. It is therefore in opposition to what are referred to as positivism and empiricism in traditional science – the assumptions that the nature of the world can be revealed by observation, and that what exists is what we *perceive* to exist. Social constructionism cautions us to be ever suspicious of our assumptions about how the world appears to be. This means that the categories with which we as human beings apprehend the world do not necessarily refer to real divisions. For example, just because we think of some music as 'classical' and some as 'pop' does not mean we should assume that there is anything in the nature of the music itself that means it has to be divided up in that particular way. A more radical example is that of gender. Our observations of the world suggest to us that there are two categories of human being – men and women. Social constructionism would bid us to question seriously whether even this category is simply a reflection of naturally occurring distinct types of human being. This may seem a bizarre idea at first, and of course differences in repro-ductive organs are present in many species, but we should ask why this distinction has been given so much importance by human beings that whole categories of personhood (i.e. man/woman) have been built upon it. Social constructionism would suggest that we might equally well (and just as absurdly) have divided people up into tall and short, or those with ear lobes and those without.

2 Historical and cultural specificity:

The ways in which we commonly understand the world, the categories and concepts we use, are historically and culturally specific. Whether one understands the world in terms of men and women, pop music and classical music, urban life and rural life, past and future, etc., depends upon where and when in the world one lives. For example, the notion of childhood has undergone tremendous change over the centuries. What it has been thought 'natural' for children to do has changed, as well as what parents were expected to do for their children (e.g. Aries, 1962). It is only in relatively recent historical times that children have ceased to be simply small adults (in all but their legal rights). And we only have to look as far back as the writings of Dickens to remind ourselves that the idea of children as innocents in need of adult protection is a very recent one indeed. We can see changes even within the timespan of the last fifty years or so, with radical consequences for how parents are advised to bring up their children.

This means that all ways of understanding are historically and culturally relative. Not only are they specific to particular cultures and periods of history, they are seen as products of that culture and history, and are dependent upon the particular social and economic arrangements prevailing in that culture at that time. The particular forms of knowledge that abound in any culture are therefore artefacts of it, and we should not assume that *our* ways of understanding are necessarily any better (in terms of being any nearer the truth) than other ways.

3 Knowledge is sustained by social processes:

If our knowledge of the world, our common ways of understanding it, is not derived from the nature of the world as it really is, where does it come from? The social constructionist answer is that people construct it between them. It is through the daily interactions between people in the course of social life that our versions of knowledge become fabricated. Therefore social interaction of all kinds, and particularly language, is of great interest to social constructionists. The goings-on between people in the course of their everyday lives are seen as the practices during which our shared versions of knowledge are constructed. Therefore what we regard as 'truth' (which of course varies historically and cross-culturally), i.e. our current accepted ways of understanding the world, is a product not of objective observation of the world, but of the social processes and interactions in which people are constantly engaged with each other.

4 Knowledge and social action go together:

These 'negotiated' understandings could take a wide variety of different forms, and we can therefore talk of numerous possible 'social constructions' of the world. But each different construction also brings with it, or invites, a different kind of action from human beings. For example, before the Temperance movement, drunks were seen as entirely responsible for their behaviour, and therefore blameworthy. A typical response was therefore imprisonment. However, there has been a move away from seeing drunkenness as a crime and towards thinking of it as a sickness, a kind of addiction. 'Alcoholics' are not seen as totally responsible for their behaviour, since they are the victims of a kind of drug addiction. The social action appropriate to understanding drunkenness in this way is to offer medical and psychological treatment, not imprisonment. Descriptions or constructions of the world therefore sustain some patterns of social action and exclude others.

HOW IS SOCIAL CONSTRUCTIONISM DIFFERENT FROM TRADITIONAL PSYCHOLOGY?

If we look closely at the four broad social constructionist tenets outlined above, we can see that they contain a number of features which are in quite stark contrast to most traditional psychology and social psychology, and are therefore worth spelling out:

1 Anti-essentialism:

Since the social world, including ourselves as people, is the product of social processes, it follows that there cannot be any given, determined nature to the world or people. There are no 'essences' inside things or people that make them what they are. Although some kinds of traditional psychology, such as behaviourism, would agree with this, others such as trait theory and psychoanalysis are based on the idea of some pre-given 'content' to the person. It is important to stress the radical nature of the proposal being put forward here. People sometimes misunderstand the social constructionist argument for cultural and historical specificity, and see it as just another way of taking the 'nurture' side in the 'nature/nurture' debate. But social constructionism is not just saying that one's cultural surroundings have an impact upon one's psychology, or even that our nature is a product of environmental (including social) rather than biological factors. *Both* of these views are essentialist, in that they see the person as having some definable and discoverable nature, whether given by biology or by the environment, and as such cannot be called social constructionist.

2 Anti-realism:

Social constructionism denies that our knowledge is a direct perception of reality. In fact it might be said that we construct our own versions of reality (as a culture or society) between us. Since we have to accept the historical and cultural relativism of all forms of knowledge, it follows that the notion of 'truth' becomes problematic. Within social constructionism there can be no such thing as an objective fact. All knowledge is derived from looking at the world from some perspective or other, and is in the service of some interests rather than others. The search for truth (the truth about people, about human nature, about society) has been at the foundation of social science from the start. Social constructionism therefore heralds a radically different model of what it could mean to do social science.

3 Historical and cultural specificity of knowledge:

If all forms of knowledge are historically and culturally specific, this must include the knowledge generated by the social sciences. The theories and explanations of psychology thus become time- and culture-bound and cannot be taken as once-and-for-all descriptions of human nature. The disciplines of psychology and social psychology can therefore no longer be aimed at discovering the 'true' nature of people and social life. They must instead turn their attention to a historical study of the emergence of current forms of psychological and social life, and to the social practices by which they are created. The complex issue of how people create and yet are created by the society in which they live is the focus of chapter 6.

4 Language as a pre-condition for thought:

Our ways of understanding the world come not from objective reality but from other people, both past and present. We are born into a world where the conceptual frameworks and categories used by the people in our culture already exist. These concepts and categories are acquired by all people as they develop the use of language and are thus reproduced every day by everyone who shares a culture and a language. This means that the way people think, the very categories and concepts that provide a framework of meaning for them, are provided by the language that they use. Language therefore is a necessary pre-condition for thought as we know it. Some psychologists, such as Piaget, believed that thought developed in the child before the acquisition of language, and most of traditional psychology at least holds the tacit assumption that language is a more or less straightforward expression of thought, rather than a pre-condition of it.

5   Language as a form of social action:

By placing centre-stage the everyday interactions between people and seeing these as actively producing the forms of knowledge we take for granted and their associated social phenomena, it follows that language too has to be more than simply a way of expressing ourselves. When people talk to each other, the world gets constructed. Our use of language can therefore be thought of as a form of action, and some social constructionists take this 'performative' role of language as their focus of interest. As pointed out above, traditional psychology has typically regarded language as the passive vehicle for our thoughts and emotions.

6   A focus on interaction and social practices:

Traditional psychology looks for explanations of social phenomena inside the person, for example by hypothesising the existence of attitudes, motivations, cognitions and so on. These entities are held to be responsible for what individual people do and say, as well as for wider social phenomena such as prejudice and delinquency. Sociology has traditionally countered this with the view that it is social structures (such as the economy, or the major institutions such as marriage and the family) that give rise to the social phenomena that we see. Social constructionism rejects both of these positions, and regards as the proper focus of our enquiry the social practices engaged in by people, and their interactions with each other. Explanations are to be found neither in the individual psyche nor in social structures, but in the interactive processes that take place routinely between people.

7 A focus on processes:

While most traditional psychology and sociology has put forward explanations in terms of static entities, such as personality traits, economic structures, models of memory and so on, the explanations offered by social constructionists are more often in terms of the dynamics of social interaction. The emphasis is thus more on *processes* than structures. The aim of social enquiry is moved from questions about the nature of people or society and towards a consideration of *how* certain phenomena or forms of knowledge are achieved by people in interaction. Knowledge is therefore seen not as something that a person *has* (or does not have), but as something that people *do* together. The way that such social practices are intimately bound up with social structure is discussed in chapter 6.

WHO CAN BE CALLED A SOCIAL CONSTRUCTIONIST?

My criterion for including as social constructionists the people that I do is that they appear to agree (either explicitly or implicitly) with one or more of the above. Working in North America, K.J. and M. M. Gergen, Shotter and Sarbin are key contributors to the field. Gergen and Gergen (1984, 1986) and Sarbin (1986) have particularly concentrated upon how people's accounts of themselves are constructed like stories or narratives, and Shotter's focus of interest is on the dynamic, interpersonal processes of construction, which he calls 'joint action' (Shotter, 1993a, 1993b). In Britain, Harré, drawing upon the philosopher Wittgenstein, has been a keen exponent of the view that language provides our ways of understanding ourselves and the world. The view that knowledge is historically and culturally specific is fundamental to the work of the French philosopher Foucault (e.g. Foucault, 1972, 1976, 1979), and he also stresses the constructive power of language. His ideas have been taken up and used in the field of discourse analysis in Britain by numerous people, including Parker (e.g. Parker, 1992) and Hollway (e.g. Hollway, 1984, 1989). Foucault's approach has been successfully adopted by Rose (e.g. Rose, 1989, 1990) to show how notions such as 'science' and 'the individual' have been socially constructed. The historical and cultural relativity of knowledge, and the way that 'truth' claims are constructed, have been taken up with enthusiasm by those who wish to give psychology a political cutting edge, such as Kitzinger (Kitzinger, 1987, 1989), Parker, Burman (e.g. Burman, 1990) and Walkerdine (e.g. Walkerdine, 1984). I also include as 'social constructionists' writers such as Potter, Wetherell, Edwards and Billig, some of whom prefer to call themselves 'discourse psychologists'. I include them since they are concerned primarily with the performative, action-oriented function of language and see accounts as constructed to achieve particular social goals rather than representing and expressing intra-psychic events (e.g. Potter and Wetherell, 1987; Edwards and Potter, 1992; Billig, 1987; Billig *et al.*, 1988). In addition, these writers in one sense hold an extreme social constructionist view. They argue that 'there is nothing outside the text', i.e. that when we talk about 'reality' we can only be referring to the things that we construct through language.

WHERE DID SOCIAL CONSTRUCTIONISM COME FROM?

Social constructionism as it is now infiltrating British and North American psychology and social psychology cannot be traced back to a single source. It has emerged from the combined influences of a number of North American, British and continental writers dating back more than thirty years. I shall give here what may be considered an outline of its history and major influences, bearing in mind that this 'history' itself is only one of many possible constructions of the events!

Sociological influences

As someone working and teaching in a multidisciplinary university department, it has been apparent to me that many of the fundamental assumptions of social constructionism have been alive and well and living in sociology for quite some time. Sixty years ago Mead (1934), writing in the USA, founded 'symbolic interactionism' with his book *Mind, Self and Society*. Fundamental to symbolic interactionism is the view that as people we construct our own and each other's identities through our everyday encounters with each other in social interaction. In line with this way of thinking, the sociological sub-discipline of ethnomethodology, which grew up in North America in the 1950s and 1960s, tried to understand the processes by which ordinary people construct social life and make sense of it to themselves and each other. But the major social constructionist contribution from sociology is usually taken to be Berger and Luckmann's (1966) book *The Social Construction of Reality*. Berger and Luckmann's anti-essentialist account of social life argues that human beings together create and then sustain all social phenomena through social practices. They see three fundamental processes as responsible for this: externalisation, objectivation and internalisation. People 'externalise' when they act on their world, creating some artefact or practice. For example, they may have an idea (such as the idea that the sun revolves around the earth) and 'externalise' it by telling a story or writing a book. But this then enters into the social realm; other people re-tell the story or read the book, and once in this social realm the story or book begins to take on a life of its own. The idea it expresses has become an 'object' of consciousness for people in that society ('objectivation') and has developed a kind of factual existence or truth; it seems to be 'out there', an 'objective' feature of the world which appears as 'natural', issuing from the nature of the world itself rather than dependent upon the constructive work and interactions of human beings. Finally, because future generations are born into a world where this idea already exists, they 'internalise' it as part of their consciousness, as part of their understanding of the nature of the world.

Berger and Luckmann's account shows how the world can be socially constructed by the social practices of people, but at the same time be experienced by them as if the nature of their world is pre-given and fixed. We could say that 'social constructionism' itself has now achieved the status of an object. In writing this book and ostensibly describing it I am contributing to its objectivation in the world. And in the future, students who read this and other books 'about' social constructionism will tend to think of it as an area of knowledge that has been 'discovered' rather than as an effect of social processes. In writing this book, then, I am contributing to what might be called 'the social construction of social constructionism'.

The emergence of social constructionism in psychology

In psychology, the emergence of social constructionism is usually dated from K.J. Gergen's (1973) paper 'Social psychology as history', in which he argues that all knowledge, including psychological knowledge, is historically and culturally specific, and that we therefore must extend our enquiries beyond the individual into social, political and economic realms for a proper understanding of the evolution of present-day psychology and social life. In addition, he argues that there is no point in looking for once-and-for-all descriptions of people or society, since the only abiding feature of social life is that it is continually changing. Social psychology thus becomes a form of historical undertaking, since all we can ever do is try to understand and account for how the world appears to be at the present time. In this paper can be seen the beginnings of the Gergens' later work on social psychology, history and narrative.

Gergen's paper was written at the time of what is often referred to as 'the crisis in social psychology' (e.g. see Armistead, 1974). Social psychology as a discipline can be said to have emerged from the attempts by psychologists to provide the US and British governments during the Second World War with knowledge that could be used for propaganda and the manipulation of people. It grew out of questions like 'How can we keep up the morale of troops?' and 'How can we encourage people to eat unpopular foods?' It also grew up at a time when its parent discipline of psychology was carving out a name for itself by adopting the positivist methods of the natural sciences. Social psychology as a discipline therefore emerged as an empiricist, laboratory-based science which had habitually served, and was paid for by, those in positions of power, both in government and in industry.

Social psychologists in the 1960s and early 1970s were becoming increasingly worried by the way that the discipline implicitly promoted the values of dominant groups. The 'voice' of ordinary people was seen as absent from its research practices, which, in their concentration on decontextualised laboratory behaviour, ignored the real-world contexts which give human action its meaning. A number of books were published, each in its own way trying to redress the balance, by proposing alternatives to positivist science and focussing upon the accounts of ordinary people (e.g. Harré and Secord, 1972) and by challenging the oppressive and ideological uses of psychology (e.g. Brown, 1973; Armistead, 1974). These concerns are clearly apparent today in the work of social psychologists in social constructionism.

Postmodernism

The cultural and intellectual 'backcloth' against which social constructionism has taken shape, and which to some extent gives it its particular flavour, is what is usually referred to as 'postmodernism'. Postmodernism as an intellectual movement has its centre of gravity not in the social sciences but in art and architecture, literature and cultural studies. It represents a questioning of and rejection of the fundamental assumptions of modernism, the intellectual movement which preceded it (and exists alongside it, generating much argument and debate) and which in many ways embodies the assumptions underlying intellectual and artistic life that have been around since the time of the Enlightenment, which dates from about the mid-eighteenth century.

The Enlightenment project was to search for truth, to understand the true nature of reality, through the application of reason and rationality. This is in sharp contrast to the mediaeval period, in which the church was the sole arbiter of truth, and in which it was not the responsiblity of individual human beings to discover the truth about life or to make decisions about the nature of morality. Science, as the antidote to the dogma of the mediaeval period, was born in the Enlightenment period. The individual person, rather than God and the church, became the focus for issues of truth and morality. It was now up to individuals to make judgements (based on objective, scientific evidence) about what reality was like and therefore what were appropriate moral rules for humans to live by.

The modern movement in the artistic world took up its own search for truth. This led to much discussion about, for example, the value of different ways of painting (was the Impressionist way better than the pre-Raphaelite way, or the Expressionist way?). This search for truth was often based upon the idea that there were rules or structures underlying the surface features of the world, and there was a belief in a 'right' way of doing things which could be discovered. Classical architecture (i.e. that of the Romans and Greeks) was based upon the use of particular mathematical proportions (for example the 'golden section') which were thought to lie at the heart of beautiful forms, and modern architecture too embodied the assumption that a good design in some way expressed the underlying function of the building.

In sociology, the search for rules and structure was exemplified by Marx, who explained social phenomena in terms of the underlying economic structure, and psychologists such as Freud and Piaget each postulated the existence of underlying psychic structures to account for psychological phenomena. In each case the 'hidden' structure or rule is seen as the deeper reality underlying the surface features of the world, so that the truth about the world could be revealed by analysing these underlying structures. Theories in the social sciences and humanities which postulate such structures are known as 'structuralist'; the (later) rejection of the notion of rules and structures underlying forms in the real world is thus known as 'poststructuralism', and the terms 'postmodernism' and 'poststructuralism' are sometimes used interchangeably. The common feature of all of these theories is that they constitute what are often called 'metanarratives' or grand theories. They offered a way of understanding the entire social world in terms of one all-embracing principle (e.g. for Marx it was class relations), and therefore recommendations for social change were based upon this principle (in this case, revolution by the working class).

Postmodernism is a rejection of both the idea that there can be an ultimate truth and of structuralism, the idea that the world as we see it is the result of hidden structures. In architecture, it is exemplified by the design of buildings which appear to disregard the accepted wisdoms of good design. In art and literature it is seen in the denial that some artistic or literary forms are necessarily better than others, so that 'pop' art claimed a status for itself and the objects it represented equal to that of, say, the works of Leonardo or Michelangelo. In literary criticism, it also led to the idea that there could be no 'true' reading of a poem or novel, that each person's interpretation was necessarily as good as the next, and the meanings that the original author might have intended were therefore irrelevant.

Postmodernism also rejects the idea that the world can be understood in terms of grand theories or metanarratives, and emphasises instead the co-existence of a multiplicity and variety of situation-dependent ways of life (sometimes referred to as pluralism). It argues that we (in the west) are now living in a postmodern world, a world which can no longer be understood by appeal to one over-arching system of knowledge (such as a religion). Developments in technology, in media and mass communications mean that we are now living in a condition where there are available to us many different kinds of knowledge (such as a variety of natural and social scientific disciplines, many religions, alternative medicines, a choice of 'lifestyles' and so on), each of them operating as a relatively self-contained system of knowledge which we can 'dip' in and out of as we please. Postmodernism thus rejects the notion that social change is a matter of discovering and altering the underlying structures of social life through the application of a grand theory or meta-narrative. In fact, the very word 'discover' presupposes an existing, stable reality that can be revealed by observation and analysis, an idea quite opposed to social constructionism.

As we shall see, the flavour of these ideas has been absorbed by much of social constructionism in the social sciences. Its multi-disciplinary background means that it has drawn its ideas from a number of sources, and where it has drawn on work in the humanities and literary criticism, its influences are often those of French intellectuals such as Foucault and Derrida. Its cultural backdrop is postmodernism, but it has its own intellectual roots in earlier sociological writing and in the concerns of the 'crisis' in social psychology. Social constructionism is therefore a movement which has arisen from and is influenced by a variety of disciplines and intellectual traditions.

WHAT ARE THE ISSUES FOR SOCIAL CONSTRUCTIONISM?

Having laid out the theoretical framework, it is now possible to see what some of its implications are. In the remainder of this introduction, I shall outline the questions that will be the concern of the rest of this book, and indicate in which chapters they will be dealt with.

The rejection of essentialism and the questioning of common-sense ways of understanding human beings is tackled in chapter 1, using the idea of 'personality' as a vehicle. The aim here is to question traditional psychology's understanding of the person

sufficiently to open the way for an alternative, social constructionist account. If essentialism is rejected, where should we look
for our explanations of human behaviour and experience? Social
constructionists focus upon language, and in chapter 2 I examine
the role of language in our thinking and our sense of ourselves
as persons. This is continued in chapter 3, when I look at the
notion of 'discourses' and their role in the construction of
social life. Different discourses construct social phenomena in
different ways, and entail different possibilities for human action.
So why do some discourses, some ways of representing the
world, appear to receive the label of 'truth' or 'common sense'?
This raises the issue of power relations, because some ways
of representing the world appear to have an oppressive or
constraining effect upon some groups in society. The relationship between discourse and power is examined in chapter 4,
but this concern with power raises a problem for social constructionism. If social constructionism abandons the idea of 'truth'
and of a reality that can be directly apprehended by human
beings, how can we be justified in saying that some people in
society are 'really' oppressed – is 'oppression' not just another
discourse, just another way of looking at the world? The gap
between reality and people's everyday understanding of the
world and their place in it is often discussed in terms of
'ideology'. The problem of the status of reality and the possible
role for the concept of ideology in social constructionism is
addressed in chapter 5.

Many believe that one of the aims of social science is, or should
be, ultimately to facilitate social change. Within the social
constructionist framework, what possibilities for social change
are there? Can individual people make a difference, or do you
have to change the structure of society? The answer to this
question partly depends on how you conceptualise the relationship between the individual and society, and this is the focus of
chapter 6. And what notion of 'the individual' are we left with
anyway? Does the person still have 'agency'? As the full impact of
social constructionism on the concepts of traditional psychology
becomes clear, it is obvious that a radically different concept of
personhood, or 'subjectivity', is offered by social constructionism
to the ones we have been used to. In chapters 7, 8 and 9, I look at
three concepts of the person as made possible by different
approaches within social constructionism.

Finally, as social scientists we must address the important question of what it might mean to practise social science within a social constructionist framework. In chapter 10, I look at the way that the theory informs (or should inform) research practice, and illustrate the kind of research (typically in 'discourse analysis') that has been performed. This chapter also includes some guidelines, in the form of 'worked examples', for how to carry out discourse analysis.

Throughout the book, I draw attention to the problematic areas in social constructionism and to the issues that need to be resolved if it is to be taken seriously as an approach to social science with useful things to say about how we might change ourselves and our lives.

A WORD ABOUT WORDS

Like any other area, social constructionism abounds with words and phrases that are unfamiliar to many people, and their meaning may be hard to grasp at first. In reading more advanced social constructionist texts, students are often confused by the terms they meet with, and I have to say that I consider a fair amount of what is written to be unnecessarily difficult and obscure. Throughout this book I have explained the meaning of terms that I think may be new to readers coming from traditional social science, particularly psychological, backgrounds. The relationship between the different terms and concepts is also a problematic one. Are all poststructuralists necessarily social constructionists? Is poststructuralism part of postmodernism? Does anti-essentialism or anti-realism make you a social constructionist? The answer to these questions is beyond the scope of this book, and in any case they are questions which are part of the debates and arguments which make social constructionism the rapidly changing, dynamic body of thinking that, currently, it is. To aid readers in their struggle for understanding, I have provided a brief glossary of common terms at the back of the book.

Chapter 1

Where do you get your personality from?

Social constructionism involves challenging most of our common-sense knowledge of ourselves and the world we live in. This means that it does not just offer a new analysis of topics such as 'personality' or 'attitudes' which can simply be slotted into our existing framework of understanding. The framework itself has to change, and with it our understanding of every aspect of social and psychological life.

The idea of 'personality' is a good place to begin, since it has a central place in our understanding of ourselves and others. It is fundamental to our concept of what it means to be a person. Social constructionism is counter-intuitive; it is precisely that which we take for granted which is rendered problematic by this approach, and with regard to our notions of personhood this means that the very idea that we exist as separate, discrete individuals, that our emotions are personal, spontaneous expressions of an inner self we can call our 'personality', is fundamentally questioned.

My aims in this chapter are, firstly, to challenge the common-sense view of personality, and in doing so to lay the way for an alternative, social constructionist, view, and, secondly, to draw attention to a number of central features of a social constructionist view of the person.

THE TRADITIONAL VIEW OF PERSONALITY

The notion of 'personality' is one which is so firmly embedded in our thinking in contemporary western society that we hardly, if ever, question it. It seems to us undeniably the case that the people we know have very different personalities, and that these remain relatively stable throughout our lives. We have in our language a great diversity of words for referring to a person's personality: generous, shy, sensitive, selfish, charming and so on – and we call upon them whenever we are asked to say what we think of a person, perhaps in writing a reference for a job or in describing to a friend someone we have just met. And these descriptions would be worthless if they simply referred to transient, short-lived characteristics. If I write to an employer and say that I consider Jane Smith to be an intelligent and ambitious person, my words would carry no weight if Jane Smith were in fact intelligent and ambitious today but dull-witted and lacking in motivation tomorrow.

So our notion of personality incorporates the ideas of individual differences (all people have their own unique combination of personality characteristics) and stability (your personality does not change radically from day to day, or even from year to year). Personality change is seen as something which only occurs as the result of some major life event ('Paul has become much less irresponsible since his father died') or as the result of some planned intervention, such as going to see a therapist for help in getting rid of excessive shyness.

Individual differences and stability are two aspects of what we mean by 'personality', then. But there is more. If I were to describe to you someone I had just met, and to tell you that they were independent, broad-minded, rash, fun-loving, blunt and gregarious, you would not have much difficulty in putting together a mental picture of the person. And if I were to suggest that you meet them, you would probably be able to anticipate how the meeting might go (you might look forward to it or dread it, depending upon your own 'personality'!). But if I were to say that this person is friendly, nervous, competent, thoughtless and warm you might have more difficulty. This is because we expect someone's personality to be consistent, to be composed of a set of characteristics which 'go together'. 'Fun-loving', 'rash' and 'gregarious' seem to go together in a way that 'competent', 'thoughtless' and 'warm' do not. So that although we think of ourselves as being made up of many personality characteristics, these are by no means a random conglomeration of diverse traits with nothing in common. What we see in ourselves and in others is a unified personality, a coherent and consistent self.

As well as these three aspects of personality – individual difference, stability and coherence – there is also a fourth important aspect, and this is the relationship of our personality to our behaviour. We usually think of this relationship as a one-way street. We think of our personality as being a very strong influence on our behaviour – what we do is the result of the kind of person we are (unless we have been coerced). Kind people help you when you are in trouble, tight-fisted ones never buy a round, and shy people avoid parties. We do not imagine the 'traffic' going in the other direction, that is, we tend not to think of our behaviour as causing or explaining our personality. We do not imagine that people become mean because they do not buy you a drink in the pub.

Traditional psychology has broadly adopted this view of personality, and psychologists have devoted many years to describing, cataloguing and measuring a great variety of personality traits. Cattell, the designer of the 16PF (16 Personality Factors) personality inventory, believed that all the traits exhibited by human beings could be reduced down to just 16 (e.g. Cattell, 1946; Cattell and IPAT staff, 1986). Any person could then be described in terms of how much of each of these 16 factors his or her personality contained. Eysenck (e.g. Eysenck and Eysenck, 1967), from whom we get the Eysenck Personality Inventory, or EPI, preferred to group together such traits broadly to form personality types. By completing an EPI a person will gain a score on two dimensions of personality (introversion/extraversion and neuroticism/stability). They can thus be described as, say, a neurotic introvert or stable extravert.

This common-sense notion of personality ('common' in that it is a widely shared idea) can be described as 'essentialist'. 'Essentialism' is a way of understanding the world that sees things (including human beings) as having their own particular essence or nature, something which can be said to belong to them and which explains how they behave (things like chairs, paper and plastic spoons do not 'behave' in the human sense of 'doing something', but they do react differently to different environmental conditions, and these reactions can be explained in terms of the things we know about the 'nature' of plastic or wood). Tables and desks are hard (a property) and therefore do not bend when you put a pile of books on them. In the same way, we think of the 'nature' of the shy person being such that it is unsuited to the conditions of a noisy social gathering.

This 'essentialist' view of personality, then, bids us think of ourselves as having a particular nature, both as individuals and as a species (ie. 'human nature'), and this nature determines what people can and cannot do. Just as you cannot expect to make a useful table out of knitting wool, so you cannot expect an impatient person to wait for you. And if we believe that the nature of the human species is essentially aggressive and self-interested, the best we can do is to ensure that society provides ways of restraining people and physically preventing them from behaving 'naturally'.

This view of personality, then, suggests that the kind of person you are is in some degree the result of your biology (perhaps inherited through your genetic make-up, through the balance of chemicals operating in the brain, or through hormones and so on). To say that a person's personality is entirely determined by biological factors is an extreme view, and one held by very few people today. Most people settle for a model of personality which suggests that these biological 'givens' are to some extent modifiable by environmental influences (such as the kinds of childhood experience you have). But the fact that we find personality change so difficult when we attempt it (perhaps you are a timid person trying to become more confident, or a 'worrier' who is trying to be less anxious) seems to give credence to the idea that, even if personality is not entirely determined biologically, one way or another, once your personality is formed your 'programming' has been fixed for the future.

To a large extent, this common-sense view of personality serves us reasonably well in our day-to-day lives. It appears to make sense of what we see around us in other people and in ourselves. However, it is not without problems, and the rest of this chapter will be devoted to pointing out some of the things that this common-sense view does not explain well. The aim here is to raise enough questions about this notion of personality to make you think that alternative explanations are worthy of consideration. And throughout the rest of the book I shall be developing one particular kind of alternative explanation, that of social constructionism ('personality' is only one of a number of psychological and social phenomena that social constructionism seeks to explain).

PROBLEMS WITH THE TRADITIONAL VIEW OF PERSONALITY

First of all, how can you be sure that you have a 'personality' at all? If I were to ask you for evidence that, say, you have brown eyes, or that you live in a second-floor flat, the matter would be settled very quickly. You could let me look at your eyes, and you could show me your flat. But can you show me your personality? Where is it? Even if a surgeon were to open you up and look, she or he would not find it. There is no objective evidence that you can appeal to which would demonstrate the existence of your personality. What this shows is that whatever this 'personality' creature is, its existence is inferred. This means that in order to account for the things you find yourself and other people doing, the ways you behave, you have come up with the idea that people have a thing called a personality that is responsible for this behaviour. This is just what physicists did with 'black holes' in space. The idea of black holes was put forward to try to explain certain phenomena long before there was any objective evidence for black holes themselves. Their existence was inferred from observations of other phenomena. But in the case of personality, you could say we are still waiting for the evidence.

What this amounts to is a kind of circular reasoning. Let me give an example. If we witness someone physically attacking another person, unless we have good reason to think otherwise (perhaps that they were acting in self-defence, or that it was an accident) we are likely to infer that the attacker is an aggressive person. This is a description of his or her personality. However, if someone were to ask us why we think the attacker did it, we are likely to say something like 'If you're an aggressive person, that's the kind of thing you're likely to do.' This is circular reasoning. We have observed the behaviour (the attack) and inferred from it that the attacker has an aggressive personality. But when asked to say what made him or her do it, we account for the behaviour in terms of the 'aggressiveness' that this behaviour itself was used to infer. We call someone aggressive because of his or her behaviour and then say it was the aggressiveness that made her or him do it, but we have had no way of establishing the real existence of this 'aggressive personality' outside of the personality–behaviour circle that we have created.

This suggests that the idea of 'personality' is one that we use in our everyday lives in order to try to make sense of the things that we and other people do. 'Personality' can then come to be seen as a theory (one held very widely in our society) for explaining human behaviour, and for trying to anticipate our part in social interactions with others. We could say that in our daily lives we act as if there were such a thing as personality, and most of the time we get by reasonably well by doing so. But it is a big leap from this to saying that personality really exists (in the sense of traits inhabiting our mental structures, or being written into our genetic material).

Another weak point in the 'personality really exists' argument is this. If personality does really exist in this way, then we are describing part of human nature. We should expect to find 'personality' as we know it in all human beings, no matter what part of the world they inhabit or what period of history they may have occupied. But it is clear that all peoples do not subscribe to our western view. In some cultures, people account for their actions by reference to invisible spirits and demons and would find our idea that behaviour originates in personality a very strange one. Many people today, as well as in the past, see their actions as the result of divine guidance, and in some circumstances, people who claim that they are directed by invisible spirits are labelled 'insane'. The uniqueness and private nature of much of what we mean by 'personality' is also not a feature of all cultures. For example, we tend to think of our emotions as private events that are bound up with the kind of people we are. A person with a 'depressive' personality might be expected to feel 'sadness' often . We imagine a 'caring' person to have 'loving' feelings. These feelings or emotions are thought of as the internal, private experience of individuals, and are intimately connected to the type of person they are. For example, anger is something we feel inside us, and which is manifested in the things we say and do. However, as Lutz (1982, 1990) has pointed out, this is not the case in all cultures. For the Ifaluk (Samoan and Pintupi Aborigine), emotion words are statements not about people's internal states but about their relationship to events and other people. The Ifaluk talk of *song*, which in translation comes out as something like 'justifiable anger'. This justifiable anger is not a privately owned feeling, but a moral and public account of some transgression of accepted social practices and values.

Of course we could claim that these cultural differences are due to differences in education and understanding. We could suggest that non-western cultures (and those of previous historical periods) do not have the benefit of our knowledge. What we would be doing then is making a claim about the truthfulness of our own view as opposed to the falsity of theirs. We would be saying 'We know that in fact people have personalities, and that the way people behave is heavily influenced by their personality. People in other cultures have not realised this yet, and they therefore hold a false view of reality.' This is to state the case rather strongly, but it makes the point that unless we have complete confidence in the 'personality really exists' view, we have to accept that personality may be a theory which is peculiar to certain societies at a certain point in time.

Some writers, such as the psychoanalyst Fromm (though he is not a social constructionist), have suggested that 'human nature' is a product of the particular societal and economic structure that we are born into (e.g. Fromm, 1942/1960, 1955). For example, in a capitalist society the keyword is 'competition'; society is structured around individuals and organisations that compete with each other for jobs, markets, etc. The assumption is that the person with the most skill, intelligence, ability, charm, etc., will succeed where others will fail. So that where competition is a fundamental feature of social and economic life, what you will get is 'competitive' people and a model of the person which is framed in terms of individual differences. In other words, we think of ourselves as individuals differing from each other along a number of personality dimensions because we live in a society founded on competition. 'Competitiveness' and 'greed' then come to be seen as products of the social and economic structure we live in rather than as features of an essential human nature.

As well as cultural differences in how people think about and describe their experiences, there are also historical differences which add weight to the argument. Our language is constantly changing and we accept that the meanings of words mutate over time. But the way in which some meanings have changed, and often quite recently at that, is of interest. The verb 'to love' is a good example. To children learning the intricacies of grammar, verbs are described as 'doing' words – they are words that tell you what people are doing, like 'working' or 'crying'. But the way in which today we employ the verb 'to love' has different connotations. When we say we love someone, what we are often referring to is our feelings for them, not our actions. And yet this

has not always been the case. When I was a child, my grand-
mother sometimes used to say 'Come here and give me a love' or
'Let me love you for a minute.' To 'love' someone here means to
embrace them physically, and perhaps to comfort them. Maybe in
some parts of the country this meaning is still used occasionally,
but in the vast majority of cases when we talk about loving
someone, we are talking about private events, our feelings, things
which are taken to exist inside us and which influence how we
treat people. 'Love' has therefore become something which is
seen as motivating our behaviour rather than as a word which
describes our behaviour. Ironically, when love is relegated to this
internal domain it can become so unrelated to conduct that it can
be used to excuse the most appalling behaviour ('I hit her when
I get angry – but I love her really . . .').

This trend towards using words to describe internal events,
like feelings, rather than actions can be called 'psychologisation'.
In other words, we are tending more and more to describe
human life in terms of psychological qualities (such as feelings
and personality traits) rather than in terms of what we are doing
with or to other people. 'Caring' is another good example. To care
for someone, in today's language, means not only to look after
them and tend to their needs, but also to have caring feelings
toward them. To be a 'caring' person today is taken to be a
description of the kind of person you are rather than of the type
of activities you are engaged in. This move towards accounting
for ourselves in terms of internal events is of course entirely
consistent with the above idea that the way people think about
themselves and represent their experience to themselves and
others is dependent not upon some pre-existing essential human
nature but upon the particular social and economic arrangements
prevailing in their culture at that time.

So far I have raised a question mark above two of the key
elements of the common-sense view of personality – the idea
that personality traits influence behaviour, and the notion of
individual differences (in traits, feelings, etc.) as trans-cultural,
trans-historical 'essences' of the person. But we still need to question the two remaining notions of 'stability' and 'coherence' in
personality.

As I mentioned earlier, one of the fundamental assumptions of
the common-sense view of personality is that personality is stable
across situations and over time. However, this does not stand up

to scrutiny when we examine our own day-to-day experience. Do you behave in the same way when you are in the pub with your mates and when you are taking tea with great-uncle Eric? (I'm sure you can find your own equivalents.) Do you talk to your closest friend in the same way as to your bank manager? Do you feel confident, outgoing and 'on the ball' when you are at a party with people you know? What about when you go for a job interview? These examples may look trivial and you will probably already be coming up with explanations for the differences. But the overall message is an important one. We behave, think and feel differently depending on whom we are with, what we are doing and why. There already exist a number of psychological and social psychological theories which, while they fall short of being 'social constructionist' in the sense used by this book, offer explanations of the person that reside in the social situation rather than within the person. For example, social learning theorists talk about the 'situation specificity' of behaviour. They suggest that our behaviour is dependent not upon personality characteristics but upon the nature of the situations in which we find ourselves. Behaviour is therefore 'specific' to a particular situation (and, social learning theorists would say, is acquired through the particular set of 'reinforcers' present in those situations). According to this view we should expect a person to be different in different situations, whereas for the traditional 'personality' view these differences are problematic. Of course it is true that when we find ourselves in a situation similar to one we have been in before we will tend to behave in the way we did before. Social learning theorists would not see this as evidence for the stability of personality traits. We are simply producing the same behaviour that has proved rewarding in the past in a new but similar situation. See Mischel (1968) for an account of social learning theory.

Social learning theory is not the only alternative to the 'personality' view that accounts for differences in behaviour across situations. Sociologists and social psychologists use the notion of 'role' to show the context-bound nature of what we do. For example, the demands of the role of 'mother' are very different from those of the role of 'committee member'. Our behaviour will vary depending upon the role that we are currently occupying or playing. However, it is important that we do not think of role-playing as pretending to be something we are not, as some kind of 'cloak' which covers over our real self (our 'personality'). For example, when I am at home with my children (in the role of 'mother') my behaviour, thoughts and feelings are certainly different to when I am delivering a lecture (in the role of 'lecturer'). However, in no sense can I be said to be 'pretending' in either situation.

Social learning theory and role theory are both accounts of how, once we have questioned the common-sense view of personality, we can begin to explain how people are different in different situations. I am including them here not as examples of 'social constructionism', but to show how the field is opened up for alternative explanations once the 'personality' view is disputed.

Just as we take for granted the idea that our personality is stable, so do we also tend not to question the notion that each person has a unified, coherent personality, a self which is made up of elements that are consistent with each other. We have already begun to question this here with the implication that people might have a number of personalities or selves, depending on the situation and whom they are with. But there is also good reason to believe that a person is never a coherent system of consistent elements. Psychologists themselves have found it necessary to come up with hypothetical structures and processes precisely because our experience of ourselves and of each other is just the opposite of coherent. We talk of being 'in conflict', we say that our thoughts lead us in one direction and our feelings in another, we say that our heart rules our head, or that we have acted out of character.

In psychoanalytic theory, conflict and inconsistency are accounted for by saying that we have an unconscious, a repository of repressed feelings that act upon us but of which we are not consciously aware. Role theorists talk of 'role conflict', the experience of trying to act out two (or more) incompatible roles simultaneously. For example, the roles of 'mother' and 'employee' give some women the feeling of almost literally being 'pulled in two directions at once'. What we have here are different attempts to explain our experiences of conflict and discontinuity, experiences which pose a problem for the traditional view of personality.

THE SOCIAL CONSTRUCTION OF PERSONALITY

What might it mean, then, to say that personality is socially constructed? One way of looking at this is to think of personality (the kind of person you are) as existing not within people but between them. This is hard to conceptualise at first, so I will give you some illustrative examples. Take some of the personality-type words we use to describe people: for example, friendly, caring, shy, self-conscious, charming, bad-tempered, thoughtless. If you like, make your own list of words you could use to describe the people you know. I would predict that most of them will be words which would completely lose their meaning if the person described were living alone on a desert island. Without the presence of other people, i.e. a social environment, can a person be said to be 'friendly', 'shy' or 'caring'? The point is that we use these words as if they referred to entities existing within the person they describe, but once the person is removed from their relations with others the words become meaningless. They refer to our behaviour towards other people. The friendliness, shyness or caring exists not inside people, but in the relation between them. Of course you could reply that, even on the desert island, a person can still carry with them the predisposition to be friendly, shy, etc. We can neither prove nor disprove the existence of personality traits, and similarly we cannot demonstrate the 'truth' of a social constructionist view simply by an appeal to the evidence. In the end our task may be to decide which view offers us the best way of understanding ourselves and others and thus of guiding our research and action (I will return to these issues in later chapters).

Next, think of a person you know, someone with whom you are more than just slightly acquainted. Think about how you are when you are with that person. Perhaps you feel that when you are with her or him you are level-headed and rational. She or he always seems to be leaping from one crisis to another and seems to be in awe of your apparent ability to take the world in your stride. The nature of the relationship between you is one of counsellor and client, or 'the strong one' and 'the weak one'. Now think of someone else with whom you are just the opposite. With this person you always seem to be pouring out your troubles, asking advice and taking the lead from him or her. Perhaps this particular example does not fit you, but you will be able to think of comparable ones. The point is that it makes no sense to ask which of these is the real you. They both are, but each version of 'you' is a product of your relationships with others. Each 'you' is constructed socially, out of the social encounters that make up your relationships. Shotter has put forward the concept of 'joint action' to try to get away from the idea that what people do and say somehow emanates from internal psychic structures such as personality (Shotter, 1993a, 1993b). When people interact, it is rather like a dance in which they are constantly moving together, subtly responding to each other's rhythm and posture. The dance is constructed between them and cannot be seen as the result of either person's prior intentions. Likewise, when we interact, our talk and behaviour is a joint effort, not the product of internal forces. Amongst other things, this can explain how, despite our best resolutions, we often end up saying and doing exactly that which we wanted to avoid doing or saying.

If your personality depends upon whom you are with, then this is certainly a problem not only for personality theory but also for how we think about person perception, a key issue in social psychology. Person perception theory is heavily dependent upon the common-sense view of personality. Very simply stated, one of the the key questions in person perception is this: how can we make an accurate assessment of someone's personality? The notion of 'accuracy' assumes there to be 'correct' and 'incorrect' accounts of what a person is really like. Try this exercise: think of three words or terms (of the personality-trait kind) to describe yourself. Now think of three that your parents might use to describe you to someone. Lastly, think of three words that your girlfriend, boyfriend or partner might use. My prediction is that there will be at least some differences between the three descriptions. But who is right? If there is only one real you, one personality, two of these descriptions (at least!) are wrong. However, the alternative view is to say that they are all right, but that each version of 'you' is a product of that relationship, something created and constructed between you. The idea of bias and error in person perception rests upon the fundamental assumption that a person has a particular personality and that it is (theoretically at least) possible to 'discover' it.

Let us now sum up the position we have arrived at. A number of assumptions fundamental to the common-sense view of personality have been challenged. Rather than view personality as something which exists inside us, in the form of traits or characteristics, we could see the person we are as the product of social encounters and relationships – that is, socially constructed. This means that we create rather than discover ourselves and other people. It is important not to mistake this for an 'environmentalist' position. Environmentalism also rejects the idea that people turn out in particular ways because of a pre-existing set of biological characteristics or some form of general 'human nature'. However, this view would accept that people do have personalities, stable characters, etc., but that these are determined, at least to a large extent, by the physical and social environments in which we grow up and live. It is therefore on the 'nurture' side of the 'nature/nurture' debate, but is deterministic and essentialist all the same.

Instead, then, of people having single, unified and fixed selves, perhaps we are fragmented, having a multiplicity of potential selves which are not necessarily consistent with each other. The self which is constantly on the move, changing from situation to situation, is contrasted with the traditional view of the stable, unchanging personality. And our view of 'human nature' becomes historically and culturally bound rather than fixed for all time. What we have traditionally called 'personality' begins to look more like a theory that we are using to try to make sense of the patterns we see in our experience rather than a fact of human nature.

One of the problems that this kind of reasoning can lead to is the feeling that we are living under an illusion. We feel ourselves really to have a 'personality', we feel as though sometimes we are hiding our 'true' self, and social constructionism seems to be saying that the person you imagine yourself to be does not really exist at all – it is just an illusion. There is some truth in this. Social constructionism certainly cautions us against taking at face value our experience of ourselves and the world, and suggests that our usual understanding of ourselves may be misleading. But in saying that you have no 'true' self, it does not imply that the selves we inhabit are therefore false. 'True' and 'false' become inappropriate ways of thinking about selfhood. It is possible to say that we have no 'true' self but that we have a number of selves which are equally real. Our experiences of ourselves are real enough, and there is a sense in which we give the concept of 'personality' real existence through the way in which we live it and act it out in our encounters with each other. Certainly, if we are going to entertain social constructionist ideas sympathetically, we need to be offered some explanations and alternative accounts of our experience of being a person. For example, it is all very well to claim that we do not have a personality, and that rather we have a multiplicity of different selves. But we still feel (at least some of the time) as though we are a single, unified self, and we need to be given some explanation of this feeling. One suggestion is that our feelings of consistency and continuity in time are provided by our memory. Memory allows us to look back on our behaviours and experiences, to select those that seem to 'hang together' in some narrative framework (literally the story of your life) and to look for patterns, repetitions and so on that provide us with the impression of continuity and coherence. What we think of as 'personality' is thus seen as an effect of memory and our search for meaning and pattern in our experiences. It will be becoming plain that what it means to be a person and how we should understand our psychology will look quite different, even strange, from the social constructionist perspective, and I will look in more detail at the nature of personhood and subjectivity in later chapters.

If we are not to talk of 'personality' as a meaningful way of understanding ourselves, what concepts are available to us instead? One that is frequently used by social constructionist writers is that of 'identity'. 'Identity' avoids the essentialist connotations of personality, and is also an implicitly social concept. When you identify something, say a plant or an animal, you give it an identity. To say 'That's a weed' or 'There's a wild animal' is not to detect some essential feature or nature of the thing you are looking at. 'Flower' versus 'weed' is a dimension only relevant if you are a gardener. 'Edible' versus 'inedible' might be the (albeit not articulable) dimension used by sheep and cows, and 'wild' versus 'tame' is a distinction that surely only has meaning for humans (since 'tame' implies an encounter and relationship with human beings). The point is that it is you that is doing the identifying, and the identity you confer has more to do with your purposes than the 'nature' of the thing itself. The same applies to the things that make up human identities, such as masculinity/femininity, hetero-/homosexual, sane/insane, black[1]/white, working-/middle-class and so on – these may be seen as socially bestowed identities rather than essences of the person, and this is why the term 'identity' is often found in social constructionist writing.

The points that I have dealt with in this chapter are important ones and will come up again many times in later chapters. The multiplicity and fragmentation of selfhood, its changeability, and its cultural and historical dependence are at the heart of social constructionist accounts of the person. You do not have to be a social constructionist to abandon traditional personality theory (as we have seen, behaviourists and social learning theorists did this a long time ago). But it is a useful starting point from which to explore the social constructionist views which have gained a foothold in social psychology in the last fifteen years or so.

NOTE

1 I use this term throughout the book to refer to non-white peoples. Although it may carry slightly different meanings for North American readers, it will be a familiar term and probably carries relatively few racist connotations.

SUGGESTED FURTHER READING

Kitzinger, C. (1992) 'The individuated self-concept: a critical analysis of social constructionist writing on individualism', in G. Breakwell (ed.) *Social Psychology of Identity and the Self Concept*, London: Surrey University Press in association with Academic Press. This is a good, clear account of the social constructionist case against the concept of 'the individual'.

Potter, J. and Wetherell, M. (1987) *Discourse and Social Psychology: Beyond Attitudes and Behaviour*, London: Sage. A key text, based upon a constructionist critique of the traditional psychological concept of 'attitude'.

Chapter 2

Does language affect the way we think?

In chapter 1, I made a case for the view that the person is socially constructed. In this chapter I shall present the view that this construction process is rooted in language. The terms 'structuralism' and 'poststructuralism' will be introduced here, together with a brief explanation of them in the context of language. In the introduction, I talked about how structuralist and poststructuralist ideas had been appropriated by some social constructionists. In particular, postructuralism is an anti-humanist and anti-essentialist theoretical approach which is therefore in sympathy with much social constructionism, and because the 'centre of gravity' of both structuralism and post-structuralism is in the humanities and linguistics, they have much to offer a social constructionist understanding of language and its role in social and psychological life.

Language is unique to human beings. Undeniably, other animals communicate with each other. Scent, sound, markings, gesture and posture are employed by animals to signal danger, occupation of territory, sexual overtures and so on, but do they warrant the name of language? These behaviours clearly do have meanings, to which other animals respond (e.g. by fighting, running away, copulating, etc.) But the difference is that these meanings appear to be fixed and stable. When a dog rolls over and displays its belly, this is a sign of submission. It has the same meaning for all dogs, and this meaning has remained stable for countless generations of dogs. As we shall see later on in this chapter, it is the insistence upon the nature of language as constantly changing and varied in its meanings that is the keystone of social constructionism. And not only this, but language is seen as having a much more important role in human life than traditional psychology has given it, to the point of saying that the very nature of ourselves as people, our thoughts, feelings and experiences, are all the result of language.

THE SOCIAL CONSTRUCTIONIST VIEW OF LANGUAGE

Our traditional, common-sense view of the relationship between language and the person sees the one as a means of expressing the other. When people talk about 'myself', their 'personality' or some aspect of their experience, it is assumed that this self, personality or experience pre-dates and exists independently of the words used to describe it. We think of language as a bag of labels which we can choose from in trying to describe our internal states (thoughts, feelings, etc.). The nature of the person and her or his internal states seem to us to come first, and the job of language is to find a way of expressing these things to other people. In this way of thinking, then, people and the language they use are certainly closely bound up with each other; people use language to give expression to things that already exist in themselves or in the world, but the two are essentially independent things.

This way of understanding the relationship between the person and language is in radical opposition to a poststructuralist view, which sees the person as constructed through language. The person cannot pre-date language because it is language which brings the person into being in the first place. This sounds rather bizarre at first. It seems as if we are saying that human beings just would not exist if they did not have language. Did cave people and their forebears not exist? But human beings, people as we know them today, inhabit a world of experience which it is hard to imagine being possible for the cave-dweller. Our daily experience is crammed with our hopes and fears for the future, our desires and worries, embarrassments and disappointments. We examine our motivations, drives and unconscious wishes. It is hard to imagine that the early humans too used these concepts to understand themselves and their world, but had not yet developed the linguistic tools for describing them to each other. The alternative is that language itself provides us with a way of structuring our experience of ourselves and the world, and that the concepts we use do not pre-date language but are made possible by it. This is very like the strong form of the Sapir–Whorf hypothesis (Sapir, 1947), which states that language determines thought and that if there is no way to express a particular concept in a language, then that concept just cannot be used by people who speak that language. This is what is meant by the phrase, used frequently by writers in social constructionism, that 'language is not transparent', i.e. we should guard against the (common-sense) assumption that language is nothing more than a clear, pure medium through which our thoughts and feelings can be made available to others, rather like a good telephone line or a window which has no irregularities in the glass which could distort one's view.

There are two implications of this. Firstly, it implies that what we take 'being a person' to mean (such as having a personality, being motivated by drives, desires, etc., having loves, hates and jealousies and so on) is not part of some essential human nature which would be there whether we had language or not. These things become 'available' to us, through language, as ways of structuring our experience. Secondly, it implies that what we take 'being a person' to mean could always have been constructed differently – and indeed we live in a world in which there is still an enormous diversity of languages and of ways of understanding personhood. The possibility of alternative constructions of the self and other 'events' in one's world, through language, is fundamental to this social constructionist view.

I will spend the rest of this chapter looking at these in a little more detail. I have suggested that our experience of ourselves, how we understand ourselves and others, does not originate in 'pre-packaged' forms inside us. For example, psychoanalysts take the view that there are discrete and identifiable emotions, such as anger, envy and hatred, which are innate in all human beings. They are part of the way human beings are 'programmed', and the words we have attached to them are simply the labels we have chosen to refer to these emotional entities. A social constructionist view, by contrast, would say that, in English-speaking cultures, the words 'anger', 'hatred' and 'envy' and the concepts to which they refer pre-date any one person's entry into the world (as an infant), and in the process of learning to talk we have no choice but to come to understand ourselves in terms of these concepts. This view would suggest that our experience of the world, and perhaps especially of our own internal states, is undifferentiated and intangible without the framework of language to give it structure and meaning. The way that language is structured therefore determines the way that experience and consciousness are structured.

Some examples will help to illustrate this point. Descartes (from whose name is derived the term 'Cartesian') radically changed the way people thought about themselves by suggesting that human experience was divided by a fundamental dichotomy – the physical versus the mental. He saw these as two separate realms of experience, with their own phenomena. For example, being in pain, eating one's dinner and feeling the cold could be said to belong to the physical realm. Dreaming, having a spiritual experience or coming up with a good idea belong to the mental realm. Although this was a novel idea at the time, it has quickly embedded itself in our language and thought, with profound consequences for how we understand our experience. The mental–physical dimension is one which is inescapable for us when we try to make sense of events. Is my headache physical (having an organic cause) or mental (either imaginary or originating in psychological distress)? Is 'depression' a physical illness or a mental illness? Can cancer (a physical illness) be cured by having 'positive thoughts'? The fact that these questions are often so difficult to answer should first of all alert us to the possibility that the mental–physical dichotomy may not be a very good way of trying to divide up at least some aspects of our experience. But more than this, it shows that once we have divided up the world in this way, we are left with conceptualising the mental and physical as separate but related. We are led to ask questions like 'Does physical illness affect your state of mind?' or 'Can positive thinking cure physical illness?' The very fact of the existence of the mental–physical dichotomy in our language and concepts spawns a particular kind of understanding of human beings, their experience and their potentialities.

Let us take another example. Homosexual ('homo' meaning 'same') practices have been known throughout history, and in some cultures homosexual love has been prized above all other forms of love. However, it is only relatively recently that the word 'homosexual' has appeared in our language as a noun rather than solely as an adjective. This means that it is now possible to talk about 'a homosexual', which is a person, rather than 'homosexual practices', which are something you do. Almost as if by magic, the linguistic trick of turning an adjective into a noun has 'created' a certain kind of person (which, by the way, can be seen as part of the general move towards seeing people in terms of what they are rather than what they do, described in chapter 1). Because we can *say* 'a homosexual', we can *think* in terms of 'a homosexual' (i.e. we can imagine the existence of certain kinds of person that we can call 'homosexuals'), and such language and thinking is inevitably lived out by us in our everyday dealings with each other.

LANGUAGE AND STRUCTURALISM

The idea that the structure of language determines the lines along which we divide up our experience is at the heart of what is referred to as 'structuralism'. In fact 'structuralism' means rather different things in different disciplines, but for our purposes we will take it as referring to the ideas which originated with Saussure's study of structural linguistics (Saussure, 1974), and which were later re-worked and extended to become 'poststructuralism'.

The key concept in Saussurean linguistics is that of the 'sign'. Signs can be thought of as the things that populate our mental life, things we may refer to, talk to others about, muse upon, try to describe and so on. 'Intelligence', 'dog', 'marriage', 'teaspoon' and 'art' are all signs, and they all have two parts to them. There is the thing referred to (dog, intelligence) and there is the word, the spoken sound, used to refer to it. Saussure gives these two parts different names – the spoken sound is the 'signifier', and the thing it refers to is the 'signified'. I have purposely included in my list of signs some rather abstract ones. 'Intelligence', 'art' and 'marriage' are different from 'dog' and 'teaspoon', in that we do not think of them as having the same kind of concrete existence or 'thingness' that dogs and teaspoons apparently have. However, they all qualify as 'signs' because in each case the 'signified' is not a concrete object, but a concept. So that when we use the words 'dog' and 'teaspoon' we are referring to the concepts of 'dog' and 'teaspoon', the meanings that these terms embody. If we watch a child in the process of acquiring language, we can see that this is so. At first, they may point to the family pet, and their parent may say 'Yes, "dog"!' 'Dog', the child repeats. Later, the child sees a cat or a pig and proudly announces 'Dog!', to which the adult might reply 'No, that's not a dog, that's a cat (pig).' Unless we believe that children truly do not notice any surface dissimilarities between these animals, we must conclude that what they are doing here is working out what features and characteristics the concepts 'dog', 'cat' and 'pig' encompass.

Saussure's major contribution was in his assertion that the link between the signifier (spoken sound) and the signified (concept) is an arbitrary one. At first sight this appears to be a rather obvious assertion. Of course we all know that there is nothing inherent in the sound of the word 'dog' that makes it a singularly appropriate label for the animal, and we only have to observe the fact that other languages use different words for 'dog' or 'pig' to be satisfied that the words we use to refer to concepts are just a convention – any word would do as long as everyone uses the same one. But Saussure is saying more than this. He is also saying that the concepts themselves are arbitrary divisions and categorisations of our experience. We have divided up our world into things we have called 'dogs', 'pigs', 'marriage', 'intelligence' and so on, and these divisions are arbitrary. It is quite possible that in some cultures separate concepts for 'dog' and 'cat' do not exist. In English-speaking cultures we have the words 'sheep' and 'mutton', and they refer to different concepts, but in French there is only one word, 'mouton'. Whatever differences we see between the concepts 'sheep' and 'mutton', as English-speakers, simply do not exist for the French. So when Saussure talks of the arbitrary linking of signifiers to signifieds, he is saying that, with the aid of language, we have divided up our world into arbitrary categories.

It is important to recognise here that 'arbitrary' does not imply 'accidental' or 'random'. The objects of our mental world do not exist 'out there' ready for us to attach our arbitrary labels to them, and although in principle our conceptual world could have been divided up very differently (and it is in this sense that the divisions we do have are arbitrary), the concepts we operate with are tied in with the kind of society we live in and are therefore not random (this is the theme of chapter 1, where I suggested that the concept 'personality' makes sense in a competitive capitalist society).

Signs themselves can have no intrinsic meaning. The meaning we give to the concept 'dog' does not reside within that concept itself; this would be a slide back into the idea that the things in our social world already exist 'out there', and are just waiting around for human beings to 'discover' them and label them within their language. The idea of making a division between things (any things) lies in the rules you use to say what makes them different from each other. Any category or concept can only ultimately be described by referring to yet other categories or concepts from which it is different. The concept 'dog' only has meaning by reference to its difference from other concepts such as 'cat' or 'table'. The meaning of a sign resides not intrinsically in that sign itself, but in its relationship to other signs. To give another example, it is not anything intrinsic to the signifier 'professional' that gives it its meaning, but rather its difference from and contrast with other signifiers of class such as 'manual worker' and 'trader'. This is what Saussure's structuralism is saying, then: language does not reflect a pre-existing social reality, but constitutes, brings a framework to, that reality for us. It is the structure of language, the system of signifiers and signifieds and their meanings as constituted in the differences between them, which carves up our conceptual space for us.

However, Saussure also believed that once a signifier became attached to a signified this relationship, though arbitrary, became fixed. This means that the words we use may have arbitrary meanings, but once words become attached to particular meanings they are 'fixed' in that relationship, so that the same word always has the same meaning. This explains how all the users of a particular language are able to talk to each other, to deal in the same currency of concepts (signifieds), by using the same words (signifiers).

But the problem with this is that it does not explain two things. It does not explain how the meaning of words can change over time, and it does not explain how words can carry numerous meanings, depending upon who is speaking, to whom and to what purpose. Some examples will illustrate this. The words 'It's been a lovely sunny day today' have one meaning when spoken by the TV weather reporter, but quite another when spoken by acquaintances who feel they cannot pass each other on the street without a polite exchange. The word 'gay' in the past used to mean 'happy and joyful' (and still can) but now also has a homosexual meaning, and the meaning we take from it depends upon the context in which it is used, who is using it and why.

LANGUAGE AND POSTSTRUCTURALISM

This is the point that writers after Saussure have focussed upon, and it is for this reason that they are referred to as poststructuralist. ('Post', in this sense, means 'coming after and adding to' rather than 'rejecting'.) This argument, that the meanings carried by language are never fixed, always open to question, always contestible, always temporary, is fundamental to poststructuralism and has major implications for our understanding of the person, her or his identity and the possibilities for personal and social change. This sounds like a rather large claim for such an apparently innocuous and insignificant piece of theory, but it leads us to a number of radical conclusions which I will spell out.

It will be helpful to begin with two points upon which structuralism and poststructuralism appear to be in agreement. Firstly, it is clear that both structuralism and poststructuralism see language as the prime site of the construction of the person. The person you are, your experience, your identity, your 'personality' are all the effects of language. This means that we can only represent our experiences to ourselves and to others by using the concepts embedded in our language, so that our thoughts, our feelings and how we represent our behaviour are all 'prepackaged' by language. Even this notion that we have three different categories of psychological event called 'thoughts', 'feelings' and 'behaviour' is itself a function of language, and it is quite possible (and I would think probable) that there are cultures and languages in which these categories are not present. For example, according to Lutz (1982) the Ifaluk have no word which translates as 'emotion'.

But this process of construction cannot be accomplished by individuals on their own. We must not lose sight of the fact that language is a fundamentally social phenomenon; it is something that occurs between people, whether they are having a conversation, writing a letter or a book, or filling in their tax return. It is in such exchanges between people that the construction of the person can take place. Every time we telephone a friend, visit our bank manager, take part in a seminar, read a magazine or tell someone we love them, we, and the other people either actively or implicitly involved in that exchange, are in the process of constructing and reconstructing ourselves. It is from all the myriad forms of language exchange between people that 'the person' emerges. I have already, in the previous chapter, suggested how we may have a variety of 'selves', each particular to and produced by certain relationships (say with our mother or partner) or social situations (for example being at a party or a school parents' evening). So I am taking this argument one step further here and saying that these different selves are produced through our linguistic exchanges (often, but not necessarily, 'talk') with other people.

This leads to the second point shared by structuralism and post-structuralism, which is their anti-humanism. Humanism refers to a set of assumptions about human beings which is central to much of western philosophy. In particular, it refers to the idea that the person is a unified, coherent and rational agent who is the author of his or her own experience and its meaning. Humanism is essentialist; it assumes that there is an essence at the core of an individual which is unique, coherent and unchanging (I have already questioned this view in chapter 1). But it also says that the individual's experience and the meaning it holds originates within the person, in her or his essential nature. 'Essential nature' here could refer to a number of things such as 'personality traits', 'attitudes', 'masculinity' and so on. Within this view, people's experience, their thoughts, feelings and behaviour, the sense they make of social events, all these arise from, say, whether they are extraverts or introverts, whether they hold prejudiced attitudes, or how masculine they are. By their insistence upon language as the fount of the meaning of experience, structuralists and post-structuralists have moved the psychological centre of gravity out of the individual person into the social realm. This means that if we are looking for explanations of the social world (either in terms of what individual people do and feel or in terms of groups, classes or societies) we should look not inside individuals, but out into the linguistic space in which they move with other people.

This anti-humanism also rejects the idea of the coherent, unified self, and this is a logical conclusion from the previous arguments. If the self is a product of language and social interactions, then the self will be constantly in flux, constantly changing depending upon whom the person is with, in what circumstances and to what purpose. The constructive force of language in social interaction ensures a fragmented, shifting and temporary identity for all of us. The subjective feeling we have of continuity and coherence can itself be seen as an effect of our language-based social interactions with other people, and is an effect which is more illusory than real.

This is the point at which the poststructuralist view of language becomes very important. As I mentioned earlier, the departure from structuralism is based on the view that meaning is never fixed. Words, sentences, poems, books, jokes and so on change their meaning over time, from context to context and from person to person. Meaning is always contestible; the meaning of a term, a passage in a book, or a question addressed to us is always 'up for grabs'. This means that, rather than language being a system of signs with fixed meanings upon which everyone agrees (as Saussure argued), it is a site of variability, disagreement and potential conflict. And when we talk about conflict, we are inevitably dealing in power relations. So with the poststructuralist view of language we are drawn into a view of talk, writing and social encounters as sites of struggle and conflict, where power relations are acted out and contested.

Let us work through these ideas a bit more slowly, with some examples. Take the question 'Does he take sugar?' (a good example because most people are familiar with it as an 'emblem' of the stereotyping of disability). Addressed to the parent of a young child, the question probably would not incite much interest. There are a number of assumptions implicit in the question. It assumes perhaps that the child is not in a position to know its own taste, or maybe to communicate it reliably to another person, or alternatively that it cannot be trusted to make a rational decision. Addressing the question to the child's parent assumes that the parent is likely to be more reliable in any or all of these respects. It also demonstrates the parent's position of power relative to the child (the parent is probably able to determine whether or not the sugar goes into the child's drink irrespective of its own wishes). So implicit in this very small question are a lot of assumptions about the nature of young children, the nature of adults and a demonstration of the power relationship between children and their parents. The meaning of this question, then, when addressed to the child's parent, would not usually (in our culture at least) be taken as insulting, demeaning or otherwise offensive. But when addressed to the wife of a blind man it certainly can be. The meaning of the question has changed because the situation and people are different.

Another example will serve to demonstrate how meanings are contestible, and how they depend upon who is speaking to whom. The following is a (fictional) interchange between a couple in a car. The woman is driving.

He: 'There's nothing coming after the blue van ... you can pull out. Oh, you've missed it now. You just keep looking the other way and I'll tell you when it's OK to go.'

She: 'Thanks – but if you'd just keep your head back I'd be able to see perfectly well anyway.'

He: 'There's no need to be like that – I was only being helpful.'

She: 'I don't really need you to help – I'm perfectly capable of getting us to the supermarket without constant instructions. I bet you wouldn't do it if I were a man.'

He: 'What's that supposed to mean? You're always complaining that I don't help you enough, and then when I do try to be helpful, you just throw it back in my face.'

She: 'You know perfectly well what I mean. If I were a man you wouldn't dream of suggesting that I'm incapable of driving down the road without your assistance. You only do it to assert your masculinity.'

He: 'That's complete rubbish, and you know it. You're just spoiling for a fight, and you drag that feminist stuff in just to score points. Well that's the last time I'm going out of my way to be helpful to you – if you don't want my help, then that's fine.'

There is very obviously a struggle after meaning here. Both parties are engaged in an effort to define what the other was doing, and to have their version of events given the stamp of 'the truth'. The meaning of these interchanges between the couple is being strongly contested. He is claiming that his words were an act of generosity, and she that they were an attempt to 'feminise' her and bolster his masculinity. He is struggling to produce for himself the identity of a thoughtful, helpful man – perhaps a 'New Man', and is fighting off the implied identity of chauvinist. She is trying to bring off her identity as a capable, thinking woman and to resist a representation of herself as in need of male advice and direction. Both parties are engaged in a linguistic struggle to build, maintain or reject the identities on offer in this situation.

If language is indeed the place where identities are built, maintained and challenged, then this also means that language is the crucible of change, both personal and social. A person may feel trapped, restricted or oppressed by his or her identity as, say, 'mother', 'homosexual' or 'mental patient'. Poststructuralist theory would see language as the major site where these identities could be challenged or changed. If our experience of ourselves and of our lives is only given structure and meaning by language, and if these meanings are not fixed but constantly changing, sought after and struggled for, then our experience is potentially open to an infinite number of possible meanings or constructions. What it means to be 'a woman', to be 'a child' or to be 'black' could be transformed, reconstructed, and for poststructuralists language is the key to such transformations.

Going back to my first example ('Does he take sugar?'), what is demeaning is the implication that the blind man stands in relation to his wife in the same way as the child does to the parent. It represents him as incapable of rational thought or communication and as relatively powerless. This representation could be contested – the blind man could say 'I usually get my own – I take two in coffee and one in tea, thank you.' Or his wife could reply 'Perhaps you had better ask him.' Both answers serve to contest the assumptions carried in the question, to reject the meanings it offers. Analysing the question in this way may even lead to a re-evaluation of parent–child relations. After 'unpacking' it, as I did above, some people may feel uncomfortable about the image of children it presents and with the relatively powerless position it gives them, and may decide in future to treat them more like adults in some situations. This is a form of 'consciousness-raising', and is one of the aims of what is referred to as discourse analysis, which I will address in greater detail in a later chapter.

All this does not mean to say that change is easy, or that we can just talk our way out of damaging identities or oppressive social relations. What people say and write is not divorced from the things they do, either as individuals or as groups (social practices), or from the way that society is organised and run (social structure), and I will have more to say later about what the relationship between language, social structure and social practices might look like. But it does mean that what we say, the way we represent things to each other, matters crucially. If language provides the structure and content of our thought, then in a fundamental way what we say is what we think. Arguments over whether the head of a committee should be given the genderless title of 'chairperson', or whether we should outlaw terms such as 'blackleg' and 'blacklist' because of their racist connotations, lose their apparent triviality in this light.

SUMMARY

The main thrust of this chapter has been to suggest that its title is ill-conceived. Rather than viewing language and thought as two separate phenomena which can affect each other, it is suggested that they are inseparable and that language provides the basis for all our thought. It provides us with a system of categories for dividing up our experience and giving it meaning, so that our very selves become the product of language. Language produces and constructs our experience of ourselves and each other, and is not the simple reflecting mirror belonging to our traditional (western) humanist philosophy. Structuralist writers have shown the arbitrariness of the way human experience is carved up by language, and that it could always have been different. There is nothing about the nature of the world or human beings that leads necessarily to the conceptual categories present in any language. But in its insistence upon the shifting, transitory and contestible nature of the meaning of language, and therefore of our experience and identity, poststructuralism has identified language as a site of struggle, conflict and potential personal and social change.

This focus upon language, and how people appear to be both constructed by it and manipulators of it, has been taken up in recent years by some social psychologists in the study of discourse, and it is to this that I now turn.

SUGGESTED FURTHER READING

Craib, I. (1984) *Modern Social Theory: From Parsons to Habermas*, Brighton: Harvester Wheatsheaf. This general text includes a number of very good chapters which critically assess structuralism and poststructuralism.

Gavey, N. (1989) 'Feminist poststructuralism and discourse analysis', *Psychology of Women Quarterly* 13: 459–475. A brief, clear overview of poststructuralist ideas as applied to feminism, together with some useful criticisms.

Sarup, M. (1988) *An Introductory Guide to Post-structuralism and Postmodernism*, Hemel Hempstead: Harvester Wheatsheaf. A good introduction to some of the key authors in the field.

Weedon, C. (1987) *Feminist Practice and Poststructuralist Theory*, Oxford: Blackwell. Although the focus of this book is feminism, it is also a very readable account of poststructuralist ideas.

Chapter 3

What is a discourse?

In the previous chapter I introduced a number of issues which will occupy us for the rest of this book. I talked about language as the basis of thought and selfhood, about the multiplicity of meanings inherent in any piece of text or speech, and about how this leads us to consider personal identity as temporary, fragmented and open to question. I suggested that our sense of ourselves as people, our identity, can be seen as constantly being sought after, contested, validated, maintained and so on through the use of language.

If it is the way that language is structured that provides us with the basis for our notions of selfhood and personal identity, we need to look at these structures and see how this is accomplished. One way of looking at how language is structured has been taken up with enthusiasm by many recent writers (e.g. Foucault, 1972, 1976; Parker, 1992; Hollway, 1984), and this is the idea that language is structured into a number of discourses, and that the meaning of any 'signifier' (for example, a word) depends upon the context of the discourse in which it is used.

The terms 'discourse' and 'discourse analysis' are increasingly common in books and articles written by people interested in giving language an important place in psychology and social psychology. However, these terms can have rather different meanings depending upon the theoretical traditions that the writers are using, and this depends in turn upon the particular issues and problems the writers wish to address. It will be useful at this point to say something about these differences.

TWO APPROACHES TO THE STUDY OF 'DISCOURSE'

The ideas that I have been drawing upon have come primarily from the French philosophical traditions of structuralism and poststructuralism, as they have recently been taken up by those interested in issues of identity, selfhood, personal and social change and power relations (e.g. Hollway, 1989; Parker, 1992; Weedon, 1987; Walkerdine, 1987). The particular conception of 'discourse' offered by these traditions is very fruitful when applied to such issues (though, as we shall see, they also lead us into some knotty problems). Some of these writers also draw upon psychoanalytic concepts in order to understand selfhood and subjectivity, and this is a matter of some debate and conflict within social constructionism. I will say more about their use of psychoanalytic theory in a later chapter.

However, other writers' interest in 'discourse' has a different focus, and consequently draws upon different traditions. A productive line of enquiry has focussed upon the performative qualities of discourse, that is, what people are doing with their talk or writing, what they are trying to achieve. While still drawing upon the idea of the essential variability of meaning in language, such work is also informed by speech act theory, conversation analysis and ethnomethodology. Research and writing about 'discourse' in this tradition focusses upon how accounts are constructed and bring about effects for the speaker or writer (e.g. Potter and Wetherell, 1987; Edwards and Potter, 1992; Potter and Reicher, 1987) or upon what rhetorical devices are used by people and how they are employed (e.g. Billig, 1987, 1991). Writers within this tradition are not particularly concerned with issues of selfhood, subjectivity or power, and therefore reject the use of psychoanalysis (or indeed any other brand of traditional psychology) in their accounts.

These different approaches are not incompatible; they simply reflect the different concerns of people working essentially under a 'social constructionist' umbrella, and I will be drawing upon both kinds of work in this book. However, since my current focus is primarily upon issues of personhood, identity and change I shall, for the moment, concentrate upon the work of those writing within structuralist and poststructuralist traditions. I will explore in more depth the nature of the differences between writers inhabiting the world of 'discourse' in a later chapter.

WHAT IS A 'DISCOURSE'?

Within this framework, then, what do we mean by a 'discourse'? Parker (1992) cautiously gives a working definition of a discourse as 'a system of statements which constructs an object' (p. 5). Like many abstract things, a discourse is difficult to define in a way that is 'watertight'. For example, if you tried to define 'play' you would soon find that someone could come up with examples of play that did not fit your definition, and yet for the purposes of common usage, people have sufficient understanding and agreement as to what is meant by 'play' for the term to be meaningfully used. In the same way, no definition of discourse is sufficient, and so I shall instead offer examples, illustrations, analogies, etc., which together will give the flavour of what is meant by this term.

A discourse refers to a set of meanings, metaphors, representations, images, stories, statements and so on that in some way together produce a particular version of events. It refers to a particular picture that is painted of an event (or person or class of persons), a particular way of representing it or them in a certain light. If we accept the view, outlined in the last chapter, that a multitude of alternative versions of events is potentially available through language, this means that, surrounding any one object, event, person, etc., there may be a variety of different discourses, each with a different story to tell about the object in question, a different way of representing it to the world.

Let us take an example to illustrate what is meant by a discourse. Foxhunting as an 'object' could be said to be represented in at least two radically different discourses. The 'foxhunting as pest control' discourse could be said to represent foxhunting as a natural method of keeping the fox population down to manageable numbers. Within this discourse, foxhunting is not immoral but is ultimately in the best interests of both humans and the fox, and its long tradition can be said to testify to its 'tried and tested' effectiveness. People drawing upon this discourse in their talk might be expected to say things like 'If it wasn't for the hunt, the fox population would run out of control' or 'The fox is a pest to farmers, who lose thousands of pounds each year in attacks on livestock.' Consistent with these statements might be a letter to a national newspaper extolling the virtues of foxhunting, or a poster advertising the annual hunt ball.

A different discourse of foxhunting could be 'foxhunting as the contravention of basic morality'. From the vantage point of this discourse, people might be expected to say things such as 'Animals have basic rights to life, just like humans' or 'The hunting and killing of animals is uncivilised and is unworthy of human beings.' You might also find photographs of foxes being savaged by the dog pack in newspapers or magazines, or of animal rights protesters carrying placards bearing slogans. These photographs too are manifestations of the discourse, even though they are not spoken or written language, because they can be 'read' for meaning in the same way and appear to belong to the same way of representing 'foxhunting' (putting the word in scare quotes serves to point to the fact that the nature of the object is contentious).

You might like to suggest further possible discourses of 'foxhunting', such as 'foxhunting as healthy outdoor sport' or 'foxhunting as pastime of the idle rich'. The point is that numerous discourses surround any object and each strives to represent or 'construct' it in a different way. Each discourse brings different aspects into focus, raises different issues for consideration, and has different implications for what we should do. So discourses, through what is said, written or otherwise represented, serve to construct the phenomena of our world for us, and different discourses construct these things (like 'foxhunting') in different ways, each discourse portraying the object as having a very different 'nature' from the next. Each discourse claims to say what the object really is, that is, claims to be the truth. As we shall see, claims to truth and knowledge are important issues, and lie at the heart of discussions of identity, power and change, and I will go into this in more detail in the next chapter.

Notice that what is absent from this account is any reference to notions such as 'opinion' or 'attitude'. I suggested above the kinds of thing that people might say about foxhunting, and to say that such statements issued from the person's opinions or attitudes would be completely opposed to a social constructionist view. 'Attitudes' and 'opinions' are essentialist concepts of the 'personality' kind. They invite us to think of structures residing inside the person which are part of that person's make-up and which determine or at least greatly influence what that person does, thinks and says (the presence of a positive or negative 'attitude' is inferred from what a person says, but the attitude itself is a hypothetical structure which cannot be directly observed). But such 'essences' have no place in a social constructionist understanding of the person, and have no status as explanations of the things people say. The concept of 'attitude' has been thoroughly addressed from a social constructionist position by Potter and Wetherell (1987). Let us be clear about the status of the things people say and write, from the perspective of a poststructural social constructionism: these things are not a route of access to a person's private world, they are not valid descriptions of things called 'beliefs' or 'opinions', and they cannot be taken to be manifestations of some inner, essential condition such as temperament, personality or attitude. They are manifestations of discourses, outcrops of representations of events upon the terrain of social life. They have their origin not in the person's private experience, but in the discursive culture that those people inhabit.

The things that people say or write, then, can be thought of as instances of discourses, as occasions where particular discourses are given the opportunity to construct an event in this way rather than that. Pieces of speech or writing can be said to belong to the same discourse to the extent that they are painting the same general picture of the object in question. Of course, the same words, phrases, pictures, expressions and so on might appear in a number of different discourses, each time contributing to a rather different narrative. To go back to the foxhunting example, the words 'Sentimentality over vermin is misplaced' could appear as part of the 'hunting-as-tried-and-tested-pest-control' discourse, or as part of the 'hunting-as-pastime-of-the-idle-rich' discourse. Words or sentences do not of themselves belong to any particular discourse; in fact the meaning of what we say rather depends upon the discursive context, the general conceptual framework in which our words are embedded. In this sense, a discourse can be thought of as a kind of frame of reference, a conceptual backcloth against which our utterances can be interpreted. So there is a two-way relationship between discourses and the actual things that people say or write: discourses 'show up' in the things that people say and write, and the things we say and write, in their turn, are dependent for their meaning upon the discursive context in which they appear.

A discourse about an object is said to manifest itself in texts – in speech, say a conversation or interview, in written material such as novels, newspaper articles or letters, in visual images like magazine advertisements or films, or even in the 'meanings' embodied in the clothes people wear or the way they do their hair. In fact, anything that can be 'read' for meaning can be thought of as being a manifestation of one or more discourses and can be referred to as a 'text'. Buildings may 'speak' of civic pride, like the town halls and factories of the industrial revolution, or of a yearning for the past as in the recent trend towards 'vernacular' building. Clothes and uniforms may suggest class position, status, gender, age or subculture and as such can be called texts. Given that there is virtually no aspect of human life that is exempt from meaning, everything around us can be considered as 'textual', and 'life as text' could be said to be the underlying metaphor of the discourse approach.

DISCOURSE AND IDENTITY

Let us now look at the implications of all this for personal identity. We have moved one step forward from the position we reached at the end of the previous chapter, where I suggested that our identity arises out of interactions with other people and is based on language. We can now say that our identity is constructed out of the discourses culturally available to us, and which we draw upon in our communications with other people. People's identities are achieved by a subtle interweaving of many different 'threads'. There is the 'thread' of age (for example they may be a child, a young adult or very old), that of class (depending on their occupation, income and level of education), ethnicity, gender, sexual orientation and so on. All these (and many more) are woven together to produce the fabric of a person's identity. Each of these components is 'constructed' through the discourses that are present in our culture – the discourses of age, of gender, of education, of sexuality and so on. We are the end-product, the combination, of the particular 'versions' of these things that are available to us. A young, black, unemployed man will have his identity constructed out of the raw materials of the various discourses surrounding age, ethnicity, work and masculinity. And the different components have implications for each other. The discourses of age, for example, represent people at various stages of life in different ways. Old age is often associated with loss (of personal competencies such as memory and motor skills, of status and power), decline and an absence of 'development'. But alternative discourses of old age can paint a picture of wisdom, respect and serenity. Similarly, youth is variously represented as the time of progress, development and change, a period of identity crisis, or a period of danger and non-conformity. The version of 'youth' that a person can live out is affected by the discourses of ethnicity, gender, class and so on that she or he is also subject to. The 'youth' who is black, working-class, unemployed and male is likely to be represented or 'constructed' out of rather different discourses of youth than the 'youth' who is white, middle-class, employed and female.

For each 'thread' of our identity, there is a limited (sometimes very limited) number of discourses on offer out of which we might fashion ourselves. For example, the discourses of sexuality on offer in our present society offer a restricted menu for the manufacture of sexual identity. Some newer, more recent discourses of sexuality are gaining ground; for example, there is emerging a variety of lesbian and gay sexualities, many of which have been consciously constructed and have been developed using a poststructuralist theoretical framework. However, two well-established discourses in particular call upon us to identify ourselves with respect to them – 'normal' sexuality (usually embodying notions of 'naturalness' and moral righteousness) and 'perverted' sexuality (which more or less includes anything else). The dichotomy of hetero- and homosexuality is overlaid on this, so that heterosexuality is usually represented as normal, natural and right, and homosexuality as perverted, unnatural and wrong (the two dichotomies are not synonymous, since some heterosexual practices are also seen as perversions). Given these representations of sexuality that are culturally available to us, we have no choice but to fashion our identity out of them. Our sexual activities (or lack of them!) can have no form of representation to ourselves or to the people around us other than in the form of these discourses, and so we must inevitably adopt the identity of 'straight' or pervert, of hetero- or homosexual: the representations or discourses of sexuality available within our language leave us with very few other alternatives. It is also worth pointing out here that the very use of the terms hetero- and homosexuality (like normal and perverted) creates the illusion that all varieties of homosexuality and lesbianism (and all forms of heterosexuality) are functionally equivalent, and that homosexuality is in some simple way just a mirror image of heterosexuality.

Surrounding any aspect of a person's life, then, are a variety of alternative discourses, each offering a different vision of what it means to be, say, young, educated, employed, disabled and so on. Sometimes there is no problem with combining identities supplied by discourses from different 'threads'. For example, a young person just entering higher education might effortlessly adopt the identity of 'student', because the prevalent discourses of youth and education have much in common. Youth as a time of development, exploration, and mental and physical agility fits well with the discourse of education which represents it as a process of self-development and preparation for adulthood. But a middle-aged person returning to education after a long period of employment or child care might be expected to have difficulties 'bringing off' the identity of student, because our usual ways of talking about and representing middle age do not include concepts of development or of mental and physical prowess. Middle aged students are faced with the problem of how they can construct a feasible identity for themselves out of the available discourses.

The discourses of 'science' and of 'gender' are also good examples of this. Science and masculinity pose few problems for each other. Science is thought of as logical, objective and value-free. Masculinity embodies rationality and an ability to keep one's emotions out of one's reasoning. The man who becomes a scientist can expect few identity problems. But for women there is a potential area of conflict or confusion. Prevailing discourses of femininity speak of emotionality, illogicality and intuitiveness – not the stuff of science. Women who want to do science are faced with the problem of how they can bring off their identity without appearing to be either 'not a proper woman' or 'a bad scientist'. The same is probably true in politics, and whatever one may think of Margaret Thatcher her identities as politician and as woman/wife/mother did not sit easily together.

For each of us, then, a multitude of discourses is constantly at work constructing and producing our identity. Our identity therefore originates not from inside the person, but from the social realm, where people swim in a sea of language and other signs, a sea that is invisible to us because it is the very medium of our existence as social beings. In this sense the realm of language, signs and discourse is to the person as water is to the fish. However, as I pointed out in the previous chapter, although identities are not fixed or determined by some essential nature, this does not mean to say that they have been arbitrarily or randomly fashioned. To say that identities are socially constructed through discourse does not mean to say that those identities are accidental. It is at this point that a poststructuralist social constructionism brings to bear a political analysis of the construction of our social world, including personal identity.

DISCOURSE, SOCIAL STRUCTURE AND SOCIAL PRACTICES

The discourses that form our identity have implications for what we can do and what we should do. Prevailing discourses of femininity often construct women as, say, nurturant, close to nature, emotional, negatively affected by their hormones, empathic and vulnerable. From this it is only a short step to the recommendations that women are particularly able to care for young children, and that they should do so, that they are unsuited to careers in top management or positions of responsibility, and that they should avoid potentially dangerous activities such as walking home alone at night or hitch-hiking. Prevailing discourses of 'the individual' paint a picture of human beings as separate, disconnected units 'naturally' differing from each other in terms of their motivation, talents, intelligence, determination and so on, so that, within a market economy, competitiveness and ambition secure the survival of the fittest, according to their natural abilities. But why do these particular versions of 'femininity' and 'the individual' enjoy such widespread popularity and acceptance? Why do some versions or ways of representing people or events appear as 'truth' and others as 'fiction'?

Discourses are not simply abstract ideas, ways of talking about and representing things that, as it were, float like balloons far above the real world. Discourses are intimately connected to the way that society is organised and run. In our society we have a capitalist economy and we have institutions such as the law, education, marriage and the family, and the church. These things give shape and substance to the daily lives of each of us. They offer us social positions and statuses: the capitalist economy makes us into 'workers', 'employers' or 'unemployed'. The institutions of marriage and the family mean that people can be married, single or divorced and they can be mothers or fathers or childless. The institution of education provides 'educated' and 'uneducated' people, and so on. Each of these ways of structuring society is put into practice every day by the things that people do, by social practices. Capitalism is being put into practice every time a worker 'clocks in' or collects a wage packet or unemployment benefit. Education is put into practice when children sit in classrooms or truant. The family is put into practice when mothers cook dinner for their husbands and children, or when they take time off work to care for a sick child. And all of these social structures and social practices are variously ensured or encouraged by the law and other state controls such as the benefits system and the laws of the church. The legal contract between worker and employer ensures the practices of clocking in and collection of wage packets. The law can punish parents if their children do not attend school. The lack of state benefits or provision of child care means that many women with children who might otherwise choose to work outside the home cannot afford to do so, and that some women who might prefer to stay at home with their children are forced to go out to work.

The discourses that form our identity are intimately tied to the structures and practices that are lived out in society from day to day, and it is in the interest of relatively powerful groups that some discourses and not others receive the stamp of 'truth'. If we accept that men, relative to women, are still in a more powerful position in society, then we can say that prevailing discourses of femininity serve to uphold this power inequality. Discourses such as 'education as a meritocracy' and career success as 'survival of the fittest' serve to justify the greater wealth and opportunity of the (relatively powerful) middle class by representing education and capitalism as unbiased, egalitarian institutions. Discourses representing education and capitalism as systems of social control and exploitation are less likely to enjoy widespread acceptance as common-sense truths. However, there are two cautions to be sounded at this point. Firstly, we should beware of coming to the conclusion that prevailing discourses are ensured their dominant position for eternity, or that other competing discourses cannot complete a successful 'takeover bid'. For example, this century has seen a gradual emergence of alternative discourses of femininity, and more recently of masculinity, which are gaining more ground. What can be said of women or men, or how they can be portrayed in stories, images and so on, is undergoing change, and these changes go hand in hand with changes in the way society is organised – paid work (and therefore a degree of financial independence) is available to more women than it was a century ago, and the traditional 'nuclear' family is no longer the predominant household form. Secondly, discourses do not simply 'map on to' particular political arrangements. The version of woman as nurturant, close to nature and empathic is also used by some feminists who wish to see the ascendency of 'feminine' ways of being, and attacks on the notion of 'madness' are used simultaneously by the anti-psychiatry movements as well as by those who wish to close down the mental hospitals and replace them with doubtful 'community care' for financial reasons.

Let us sum up the position so far. We have taken up the idea that all the 'objects' of our consciousness, including our 'self', our notion of what it means to be a person, and our own identity, are all constructed through language, and that it is discourses as coherent systems of representation that produce these things for us. As Parker puts it, 'A strong form of the argument would be that discourses allow us to see things that are not "really" there, and that once an object has been elaborated in a discourse it is difficult not to refer to it as if it were real' (Parker, 1992: 5). Objects such as 'intelligence', 'marriage' or 'love' are good examples – their existence has been brought about by the things people do and say, like developing 'intelligence tests' or describing how they 'fell in love', but we tend to treat them as if they had the same kind of existence as physical objects.

We have looked at the relationship between social structures, social practices and discourses, and suggested that particular discourses, particular ways of representing events and people, enjoy widespread acceptance in the form of common sense or 'truth' because such discourses are in the interests of the relatively powerful groups of society. However, illuminating though this idea is, we should not accept it uncritically. For instance, how are we to recognise a 'prevailing discourse'? By whose criteria? How can we be sure that we have correctly identified the people or groups in society whose interests they serve? Can we be sure that we are not simply dressing up, in intellectual jargon, our own common sense as social theorists? These matters have not been sufficiently addressed by researchers in social constructionism, who often appear to depend solely upon their own intuition in the identification of discourses, and have drawn some criticism on that account (e.g. Potter *et al.*, 1990). I will look at these problems in more detail in chapter 10.

The discourses we employ often have political implications that we should investigate if we are interested in changing ourselves or the world we live in. I shall look in more detail at the issue of discourse and power in the next chapter, but before we move on we ought to pay some attention to a couple of the 'knotty problems' that are lurking beneath the surface of what I have been saying in this chapter.

PROBLEMS: PERSONHOOD, AGENCY AND REALITY

If you are not already reeling from the onslaught that I have been making upon long-cherished assumptions about human life, let me now state the social constructionist case in its most extreme form. You may have been saying to yourself 'OK, so language is more important than psychologists might have thought, but this is beginning to sound as though language is all there is.' This is exactly what the extreme version of this view is saying. All the objects of our consciousness, every 'thing' we think of or talk about, including our identities, our selves and those of other people (whatever 'self' may mean), are constructed through language, manufactured out of discourses. Nothing has any essential, independent existence outside of language; discourse is all there is. The French poststructuralist philosopher Foucault (whom we will hear more about in the next chapter) put it quite simply. Discourses are 'practices which form the objects of which they speak' (Foucault, 1972: 49). A discourse provides a frame of reference, a way of interpreting the world and giving it meaning that allows some 'objects' to take shape. Going back to the example I gave in the previous chapter, 'weeds' and 'flowers' only have an existence as different objects by the application of language, by viewing plant life through a particular pair of spectacles (which we might label the 'gardening' discourse or the 'agriculture' discourse). Even 'plant life' as distinguishable from, say, 'animal life' exists only within the frame of reference of language.

Now all this presents us with two of the 'knotty problems' I mentioned earlier, and they have to do with the nature of personhood and personal agency. Firstly, we are accustomed to thinking of ourselves as having a certain kind of personality, as holding beliefs and opinions, of making up our minds about how the world works or how it should work, and we are used to assuming that our ideas, experiences, opinions and beliefs, upon which we act, have originated in our own minds – we are their 'author'. We also assume that we exercise choice and make decisions, and that, within the limits of our practical circumstances, we fashion our own lives and take responsibility for the kind of person we have become. All of this is laid open to serious question within this extreme view of language and discourse. I have already, in previous chapters, suggested that we cannot think of ourselves as having 'personalities', or a unified, coherent self, and now I am throwing out other psychological 'properties' such as attitudes and opinions, and saying that all of these 'things' are only present in discourse, they have no existence beyond language, they are an effect of language. Well, what about the rest of the 'contents' of the person as we know it? What about drives, motivations, emotions and so on? These meet with the same fate. We experience ourselves as if these things had a concrete existence in the world, but they are all brought into being through language. They are examples of objects formed through discourses. Terms such as 'personality', 'attitude', 'skill', 'temperament' and so on present a particular vision of humankind. Through the use of these terms we are invited to think of human beings as if they were endowed with varying amounts of different qualities, whether inborn, acquired through life experience or learned. Together they contribute to what might be called the discourse of individualism, a way of talking about, writing about or otherwise representing people as unique combinations of psychic material which determine the kind of life a person is likely to lead. A 'nurturant' person may well end up caring for children or taking up a career in nursing, and a white person with 'racist attitudes' might be expected to decide where to live according to the likelihood that black people might come to live next door. But, according to the social constructionist view I have been outlining, these 'qualities' only exist within the discourse of individualism – this discourse makes it possible for us to think in terms of personalities and attitudes, it brings these phenomena into view for us, but the words do not in themselves refer to real entities or psychological properties.

This means that, to all intents and purposes, we are left with an empty person, a human being with no essential psychological properties (at least none that we would find recognisable), and this is the first problem. It is certainly the case that we feel ourselves to be the bearers of personality traits, to be the holders of attitudes, and to experience emotions, drives and motivations. Our subjective experience needs to be explained, and we need to find alternative kinds of explanation for the phenomena that have previously been the domain of concepts like 'personality', 'emotions' and 'opinions'. For example, how can we explain why some people show emotion more readily than others, or why they become mentally ill? Why do some people hunt foxes and others try to stop them? What is happening when we 'fall in love'? We can no longer draw upon traditional psychological concepts, but appear to have put nothing in their place. To some extent, the social constructionist view answers this with the idea that our subjective experience is provided by the discourses in which we are culturally embedded. Going back to an example I gave earlier, our language provides the categories of 'mind' and 'body', and we talk, think and experience ourselves as if this dichotomy were a concrete reality. It is as if we internalise the ways of representing human life present in discourses (like the discourse of the 'individual') and our subjective experience flows from that. It is a complete reversal of our common-sense understanding, in which our subjective experience comes first and we then describe it and label it with language. Language (in the form of discourses) provides our subjective experience of the world. However, this claim does not really answer in detail questions like the ones I have posed above, and I think it is a fair criticism of this kind of social constructionism that the nature of personhood and subjectivity is left with a question mark hanging over it. It is a question that I will return to in later chapters.

To return to the two 'knotty problems' I spoke of, the second of these is the problem of human agency. If people are products of discourse, and the things that they say have status only as manifestations of these discourses, in what sense can we be said to have agency? The actions, words and thoughts of human beings appear to be reduced to the level of by-products of bigger linguistic entities of which we may be largely unaware. Our hopes, desires and intentions become the products of cultural, discursive structures, not the products of human agents. And not only are we unaware of this state of affairs, but we continue in the belief that human beings can change themselves and the world they live in through the force of their (apparently) independently developed and freely chosen beliefs and acts. We look around us and see the world changing, and imagine that human intention and action is at the root of it, but this is an illusion.

There is a real danger that we can become paralysed by the view that individual people can really do nothing to change themselves or their world. The problem of how human agency might be addressed within a social constructionist framework has not been neglected, but neither has it been resolved. Again, I will return to this issue later, when I will discuss more fully how we might re-conceptualise personhood and subjectivity.

A further problem with this view is how you conceptualise reality and truth. The claim that 'discourse is all there is' is a logical conclusion of the argument that language does not label discrete entities in the real world that exist independently of it. All that language can do, then, is to refer to itself. Language is a 'self-referent' system. This means that any 'sign' can only be defined in terms of other signs existing in the same language system. For example, if I was asked to define 'a tree', I could only do this by contrasting the concept 'tree' with other concepts, to demonstrate the category. I could say 'A tree is living (rather than inanimate), but not sentient like an animal, and is different from a shrub in that it has one main stem.' But all I am doing here is referring to other signs (animate, sentient, shrub) which themselves can only be defined in terms of yet more signs from the same language system. There is no way out of this into the 'real' world that might exist beyond language. Whatever the nature of the 'real' world, we cannot assume that the words in our language refer to it or describe it. The extreme form of the argument would be that things are only 'real' to the extent that discourses exist which describe them. Given that there are numerous and conflicting discourses surrounding any 'object', we are left with no notion of 'truth' (i.e. the discourse that can be said to describe the object correctly, all the others being false). All we have is a variety of different discourses or perspectives, each apparently equally valid. This is referred to as the problem of 'relativism'. The claims of each discourse are simply relative to each other, and cannot be said to be either true or false when compared to 'reality'.

This gets us into difficulties if we want to say that things like the economy, or our bodies, are real and have real effects independent of language. It also creates difficulties if we want to say that discourses which describe women (or black people or the working class) as oppressed are more valid than other discourses. The relativism which looms over this view of discourse is a minefield, and some writers prefer to conceptualise discourse as a very powerful formative influence upon our thought and experience but falling short of entirely constituting that experience for us. I intend here not to try to offer a solution to these problems, but to point to them as highly contentious theoretical and philosophical issues which are by no means clearly worked through in the discourse literature.

These problems of truth, agency, choice and their implications for personal and social change will come up throughout the rest of this book. In the next chapter, I look at how the relationship between discourse and power has been conceptualised, and the implications that this has for identity, personal agency and change.

SUGGESTED FURTHER READING

Lalljee, M. and Widdicombe, S. (1989) 'Discourse analysis', in A. M. Coleman and J.G. Beaumont (eds) *Psychology Survey 7*, London and Leicester: British Psychological Society and Routledge. A clear account of the 'speech act' variety of discourse, using good examples.

MacDonnell, D. (1986) *Theories of Discourse: An Introduction*, Oxford: Blackwell. Starting from 'the demise of structuralism', MacDonnell traces the rise to prominence of discourse theory and particularly looks at the issues of ideology and the discourse/reality problem.

Parker, I. (1992) *Discourse Dynamics: Critical Analysis for Social and Individual Psychology*, London: Routledge. Though not a particularly accessible book to students without a multidisciplinary background, this text includes a useful account of the nature of discourses. It also tries to resolve some of the difficult problems in the area, such as agency and the relationship between discourse and reality, as well as providing an extensive guide to the discourse literature.

Shotter, J. and Gergen, K.J. (eds) (1989) *Texts of Identity*, London: Sage. A rich collection of chapters by key writers in the social constructionist field (e.g. Gergen, Harré, Parker, Kitzinger, Shotter and Rose), including several specifically concerned with discourse, identity and power.

Chapter 4

What does it mean to have power?

If we now build upon some of the ideas to emerge from the previous chapters, we can begin to see that discourses are embedded in power relations, and therefore have political effects. If our identities are not fixed and pre-given, but formed through the representations available to us in discourse, then why is it that some identities 'stick' to us and others are hard to 'bring off'? The social constructionist view suggests that a large part of the answer to this lies in the fact that representations of people (e.g. as 'free individuals', as 'masculine' or as 'well-educated') can serve to support power inequalities between them, while passing off such inequalities as fair or somehow natural. Power can be thought of as the extent of a person's access to sought-after resources, such as money, leisure time, rewarding jobs, and as the extent to which they have the capacity to have some effect on their world, for example by belonging to important decision-making bodies such as the cabinet, the judiciary or the board of directors of a big company, and therefore to have some impact upon other people's lives. It is clear, then, that according to this definition some groups of people in society have less power than others. We can therefore say that (for example) the middle class has more power than the working class, that white people hold more power than black people, and that men are more powerful than women.

Although these structural inequalities are very real, they are only part of the story. As I pointed out in the previous chapter, social constructionism is not limited to an interest in language and discourse, because social structure, social practices and their associated discourses are seen as all part of the same phenomenon. To understand the power inequalities in society properly, we need to examine how discursive practices serve to create and uphold particular forms of social life. If some people can be said to be more powerful than others, then we need to examine the discourses and representations which uphold these inequalities.

The relationship between power and discourse has received a great deal of attention from writers within a poststructuralist tradition in recent years, and one of the most influential figures is that of the French philosopher Foucault. It is worth spending a little time fleshing out some of Foucault's main ideas, since they have been taken up with such enthusiasm by many writers wishing to import poststructuralist ideas into social psychology, in particular his view of the relationship between knowledge and power. Our common-sense understanding of the relationship between knowledge and power is the notion that knowledge increases a person's power. For example, by gaining the knowledge offered by higher education, a person improves his or her access to good jobs, good pay and high status. But Foucault's conception of the relationship between knowledge and power is quite different from this, as we shall see.

FOUCAULT AND POWER

I have already gone into detail about how a discourse analysis of the world puts forward the view that events, people, social phenomena and so on are subject to a variety of possible constructions or representations. Some constructions will have a greater tendency to be seen as 'common-sense' or 'truthful' than others, though this can be expected to vary greatly with the specific culture, its location in history and the structure of its society. For example, in contemporary western societies it is commonplace for the 'versions' of natural events provided by science and medicine to be given greater credence (to be given the stamp of 'truth') than those offered by religion, magic or superstition. However, this certainly has not always been the case, and is not true of all cultures in the world. Behaviour which a few hundred years ago would have been taken as evidence of 'possession by evil spirits' is today thought of as 'mental illness'. Even where scientists have not been able to put forward adequate accounts of phenomena, as in the cases of 'psychokinesis' and 'mind-reading', these things are often taken to have an underlying rational explanation which science, given time, will uncover. What we call 'knowledge' then simply refers to the particular construction or version of a phenomenon that has received the stamp of 'truth' in our society. Even within the discourse of science, what we may regard as the truth with respect to, say, a healthy diet, adequate parenting or disease prevention has changed markedly over a short timespan, and such changes cannot simply be seen as the result of progress in medical science.

For Foucault, knowledge, the particular common-sense view of the world prevailing in a culture at any one time, is intimately bound up with power. Any version of an event brings with it the potential for social practices, for acting in one way rather than another, and for marginalising alternative ways of acting. In the example above, 'evil spirits' can be 'exorcised', but 'mental illness' may require 'treatment' in a mental hospital. What it is possible for one person to do to another, under what rights and obligations, is given by the version of events currently taken as 'knowledge'. Therefore the power to act in particular ways, to claim resources, to control or be controlled depends upon the 'knowledges' currently prevailing in a society. We can exercise power by drawing upon discourses which allow our actions to be represented in an acceptable light. Foucault therefore sees power not as some form of possession, which some people have and others do not, but as an effect of discourse. To define the world or a person in a way that allows you to do the things you want is to exercise power. When we define or represent something in a particular way we are producing a particular 'knowledge' which brings power with it. To construe the world in terms of those people who are 'mad' and those who are 'sane' (thereby producing one particular 'knowledge') brings with it a power inequality between those groups. For Foucault, knowledge is a power over others, the power to define others.

Given that there are always a number of discourses surrounding an event, each offering an alternative view, each bringing with it different possibilities for action, it follows that the dominant or prevailing discourse ('knowledge' or 'common sense') is continually subject to contestation and resistance. For Foucault, power and resistance are two sides of the same coin. The power implicit in one discourse is only apparent from the resistance implicit in another.

If power is what you exercise in drawing upon discourses, Foucault's view of power, then, certainly has nothing in common with the idea that power is in evidence when one person can force others to do what she or he wants them to, that is, when their resistance is overcome. Sawicki (1991), elaborating upon Foucault's views, points out that repression and the need to resort to force is rather to be taken as evidence of a *lack* of power; repression is used when the limits of power have been reached.

DISCIPLINARY POWER

Foucault therefore rejects the view of power as an essentially repressive force, seeing it instead as at its most effective when it is productive, when it *produces* knowledge. In particular, he believes that over the last hundred years or so we have seen the rise of a number of institutional and cultural practices that have as their product 'the individual' that we know today. Changes in the nature of society, such as increases in population, the change from an agricultural to an industrial economy and so on, brought with them social practices which allowed certain discourses (or knowledges) of the person to rise to prominence. These discourses have 'produced' the individual of contemporary western industrial society; the person we feel to be inhabited by drives and motivations, possessed by traits and characteristics, and whose freely chosen actions are monitored by conscience. And these knowledges are very powerful, in that they manage the control of society and its members efficiently and without force, through what he calls 'disciplinary power'.

Foucault (1976) demonstrates how this came about. He argues that in the eighteenth century, due to the growth in numbers of people and the consequent problems of public health, housing conditions and so on, there began to emerge the concept of 'population'. Until then, those living under the rule of the monarch might have been thought of as 'a people' or 'loyal subjects', but the idea of a country having a 'population' had different implications. 'Population' brings with it estimates of the country's manpower, its organisation and the wealth it is capable of generating. It raises issues of population growth and the resources needed for meeting that growth. In short, the concept of population was a relatively sophisticated way of conceptualising the inhabitants of a country that brought with it questions of management and control. Foucault sees the body, and especially sexuality, as a major site of power relations, and describes how this came about as follows:

> At the heart of this economic and political problem of popu-
> lation was sex: it was necessary to analyse the birth-rate, the age
> of marriage, the legitimate and illegitimate births, the precocity
> and frequency of sexual relations, the ways of making them
> fertile or sterile, the effects of unmarried life or of the prohibi-
> tions ... Things went from ritual lamenting over the unfruitful
> debauchery of the rich, bachelors and libertines to a discourse
> in which the sexual conduct of the population was taken both
> as an object of analysis and as a target of intervention.
>
> (Foucault, 1976: 25–26)

In other words, sex became an area of intense interest to the state.
Those in positions of authority, in the state or the church, took on
the role of 'inquisitors' and had the power to extort confessions
about sexual practices from the men and women under their
supervision. One of the interesting points about Foucault's
analysis here is that it was only at this point that the ideas of 'sexual
perversion', 'unnatural practices' and 'sexual immorality' became
a possibility. With the power to say which practices were permis-
sible and which not inevitably came the idea of 'normality'. The
practice of scrutinising the population's sexual behaviour and of
encouraging people to confess their sexual 'sins' developed into
a powerful form of social control as people began to internalise
this process. Thus, people were encouraged to scrutinise their
own behaviour, to ask questions about their own 'normality' and
to adjust their own behaviour accordingly. The powers of the
inquisitor, the power to encourage self-examination and confession, have now passed into the hands of the present-day bearers
of authority, such as the medical profession and psychiatrists in
particular. Discourses such as psychoanalysis view sexuality as the
key to self-understanding. They encourage us to believe that in
order to resolve our personality and relationship problems, we
must discover the true nature of our sexuality. In this way personal
life is 'psychologised', and thus becomes a target for the intervention of experts.

Foucault completely reverses our usual understanding of
sexuality in the nineteenth century. The present-day orientation
towards 'sexual liberation' is commonly thought to be a reaction
against earlier sexual repression, against a time when sex was not
spoken about or otherwise openly represented in social life. This
era is usually thought of as a time when there was a pervasive

silence on the subject of sex. Foucault regards this 'repressive hypothesis' as a myth. Instead, he says that the nineteenth century saw an explosion in discourses of sexuality. Never before was sex so much scrutinised, classified, theorised and controlled. The fact that sex was not mentioned in polite society does not alter the fact that, in a diversity of ways, sexuality was rapidly being discursively constructed during this period. For example, the practice of covering the 'legs' of furniture spoke volumes about sexuality as a powerful, shameful force.

From this perspective, the nineteenth-century burgeoning of the 'sexology' literature is seen less as an increase in knowledge about sexuality than as a proliferation of classifications and divisions with which the population could be categorised and controlled. And it was not only in the area of sexuality that such a move towards surveillance and normalisation was taking place. Psychiatry developed the category of sane/insane, later extending this to innumerable varieties of abnormality (psychosis, neurosis, manic depression, schizophrenia, etc.). The development of criminology transformed crime into the study of 'criminals', certain kinds of person who were predisposed to criminal behaviour. The power of surveillance as a method of social control is epitomised, according to Foucault (1979), by Bentham's 'Panopticon'. This was a nineteenth-century invention in which prison cells were arranged around a central watch tower. From this chamber, a supervisor could keep a watchful guard over the inmates. In their cells, no prisoners could be certain that they were not being observed, and so they gradually began to police their own behaviour. Foucault's point here is that, as with the 'confessional', the practice of surveillance became internalised by those who were watched (in theory all members of society), who came to monitor and control their own behaviour according to the prevailing standards of 'normality'. This is essentially what we mean today by 'self-discipline'. Sarup (1988), in a very clear and readable brief account of Foucault's ideas, draws a worrying parallel between the Panopticon and the computer-monitoring of individuals in advanced capitalism.

Thus Foucault believes that there has been a radical shift in the way that western societies are managed and controlled. This has been a shift away from 'sovereign power', in which the sovereign controlled the populace by the power to punish, coerce or kill them, and towards 'disciplinary power', in which people are disciplined and controlled by freely subjecting themselves to the scrutiny of others (especially 'experts') and to their own self-scrutiny. Such disciplinary power, he believes, is a much more effective and efficient form of control.

DISCIPLINARY POWER AND PSYCHOLOGICAL SCIENCE

Looked at against this background, the position of psychology itself becomes highly dubious. In this light, the practice of psychology becomes seen not as a liberatory project (in which 'knowledge' discovered about human beings is used to improve their lives), but as one more cog in the machine of social control. The practice of surveillance requires information about people. This information can then be used to establish norms for 'healthy' or 'morally acceptable' behaviour, against which any person can be assessed or assess himself or herself. The history of psychology is littered with such products: intelligence tests, personality inventories, tests of masculinity, femininity and androgyny, child development tests, measurements of attitudes and beliefs and so on. All this information about ourselves constitutes, from a Foucauldian perspective, the production of knowledges which can be used to control people while making it appear as though it is in their own interests, and with the stamp of 'science' to give such knowledges authority. Rose (1990) undertakes a Foucauldian analysis of the rise of psychology as a social science and demonstrates the way that psychology is implicated in modern forms of disciplinary power.

If we take this view seriously, we must take a close look at the practice of psychology and ask how we might do things differently, and I will address this issue in a later chapter.

THE ARCHAEOLOGY OF KNOWLEDGE

It is important to note that Foucault certainly does not see the emergence and rise to prominence of particular discourses or knowledges as the result of intentional machinations by powerful groups. Powerful people do not, as it were, 'think up' and then disseminate discourses that serve their purposes. Rather, the practical and social conditions of life are seen as providing a suitable culture for some representations rather than others, and the effects of these representations may not be immediately obvious or intended. Nevertheless, once a discourse becomes available culturally, it is then possible for it to be appropriated in the interests of the relatively powerful. Historically, then, we can trace back the emergence of a discourse into a culture and try to uncover the social, physical and economic changes that provided the breeding ground for it, but we should be careful not to tie these into a causal relationship. Foucault cautioned against seeing certain social conditions as necessarily producing particular discourses. One could always look back and see how a particular discourse had emerged, but one could not look into the future and postulate that certain types of future society would be accompanied by any specific representations of human life. He was therefore opposed to the wholehearted recommendation of some discourses rather than others on the assumption that they would be more likely to bring about a better society. He saw the possibilities for the appropriation of discourses as being entirely unpredictable and their possible future effects as open ended. He refused to make any universal political or moral judgements, and this was in part because he saw that, historically, what looked like a change for the better has sometimes turned out to have undesirable consequences. His prime focus was therefore upon what he called the 'archaeology of knowledge', which entailed this tracing back to uncover the conditions which allowed a certain discourse or knowledge to emerge. His point was that if we can understand the origins of our current ways of understanding ourselves, we can begin to question their legitimacy and resist them. In doing this, he also aims to bring to the fore previously marginalised discourses, to give voice to those whose accounts of life cannot be heard within the prevailing knowledges – the voices of the mad, the delinquent, the abnormal, the disempowered. These marginalised voices and discourses are seen as important sources of resistance for us all in challenging the legitimacy of the prevailing 'knowledges' through which we understand ourselves and our lives.

By using this 'archaeology' as a method of analysis, Foucault has produced some startling insights into such institutions as the clinic and the prison. He has in effect thrown out our long-standing assumptions concerning how one goes about academic enquiry, but he has been criticised for not putting anything in their place. He offers no concrete guidelines for how one should conduct such an archaeology, or for how we should recognise a valid one when we see it. We therefore have no standards by which to judge such work, and no procedures by which we can say whether the analysis of one 'archaelogist' is better or more accurate than that of another. As we shall see later, this is a problem which dogs much of the current research which uses discourse analysis as a mode of enquiry.

Let us sum up the features of Foucault's thinking that have been discussed so far. If we think of knowledge as one possible account of events, but one which has received the stamp of 'truth', then to the extent that this version brings with it particular possibilities for acting in the world, it has power implications. For Foucault, then, knowledge and power always go together as a pair. Where there is knowledge, there is power. The two are so inseparable that they are often written as 'power/knowledge' or referred to as the 'power/knowledge couple'. Conceptualised in this way, power is not a property of any person or group, but is something that you (in theory anybody) can exercise through discourse.

This means that we should be wary of seeing power as residing in a particular group of people or institution (such as the middle class, men or the state), as power resides everywhere. Foucault was therefore quite opposed to Marxism, which sees power as lying in the hands of capitalist employers, or any other 'grand theory' for that matter. His point was that in making broad generalisations of this kind we tend to mask the vast array of differences between people and their situations and the many different kinds of power relation in which they are caught up. We risk leaving the varied 'local' power struggles between people unnoticed in our pre-occupation with what he calls 'totalising discourses'. One of the implications of this, which I will take up later, is that some power at least is available for exercise by each and every one of us, and we can use this power in our struggle to change our selves and our lives. In fact power and resistance are another 'pair' that always go together for Foucault. Prevailing discourses are always under implicit threat from alternatives which can dislodge them from their position as 'truth'. In fact you could say that if it were not for this resistance there would be no need to re-affirm constantly the truthfulness of these discourses. For example, if the notion that 'a woman's place is in the home' were really secure in its position as prevailing truth, there would be no need to keep asserting it. This opens up for people at least the possibility of change through resistance.

Foucault recommends that in order to take advantage of the unstable nature of knowledge and power, we need to be made aware of how we came to see ourselves as we do. This involves what he calls the 'archaeology of knowledge', and using this approach Foucault has himself come up with some original ideas about the development of institutions such as prisons, asylums and schools. In particular, as mentioned above, he believes that in relatively recent history there has been a shift from 'sovereign power' to 'disciplinary power', in which the population is effectively controlled through their own self-monitoring processes. This form of power is so efficient because people enter into the process willingly. It is therefore based on the assumption that people do not recognise that they are being controlled, believing their self-monitoring and surveillance to be their own choice and for their own good. Psychology itself is implicated here, to the extent that it has provided various ways of assessing and categorising people which can then be used to create norms for, say, 'well-balanced personalities' or 'socially desirable behaviours'.

These ideas about power have been taken up by many social constructionist writers (for example Weedon, 1987; Henriques *et al.*, 1984; Hollway, 1989), and I will now give some examples of how power has been thought to operate through discourse.

DISCOURSE, POWER AND IDENTITY

One of the key points raised in the last section is the idea that although the discourses which provide a framework to people's everyday experience of themselves and their lives serve purposes of social control, this process is not recognised by us as such. The argument appears to be that, on rational grounds, if people really understood that they were being controlled they would not stand for it. Foucault saw this as an essential aspect of the operation of power: 'Power is tolerable only on condition that it mask a substantial part of itself. Its success is proportional to its ability to hide its own mechanisms' (Foucault, 1976: 86).

So discourses offer a framework to people against which they may understand their own experience and behaviour and that of

others, and can be seen to be tied to social structures and practices in a way which masks the power relations operating in
society. Let us take a couple of examples to see what this might
look like. The examples come from feminist social constructionist
writing, which has been at the forefront of attempts to use these
ideas.

The discourse of 'romantic love' is one which we are all subject
to. We are surrounded by film and TV images of true love, young
love, adulterous love, love at first sight, and unrequited love.
Singers sing of it, magazines publish letters about it, and all of us
at some time have asked ourselves the question whether we are
'in' it, ever have been or ever will be. As a way of formatting our
thoughts, emotions and behaviour, the discourse of romantic love
must surely be one of the most prevalent in modern society. What
are the images and assumptions of this discourse? What does it
say? Firstly, it represents itself as a 'natural' feature of human
nature, and one that has a function in (almost exclusively heterosexual) bonding. Love appears as the emotional cement which
strengthens the sexual relationship between men and women. If
we really love someone, it means that we care about her or him
and her or his welfare, and that we to some extent bear responsibility for that welfare. It also means that sexual services can be
expected to form part of the relationship, and that these are freely
given. Secondly, love is the foundation for marriage and family
life, and marriage is seen as the appropriate and natural culmi-
nation of a romantic alliance. 'Falling in love' is therefore seen as
the precursor to a 'caring', sexual relationship (marriage) in
which men and women take responsibility for each other's
welfare and that of their family (see Averill, 1985, for a social
constructionist analysis of 'love').

However, as discourses 'romantic love', 'marriage' and 'the
family' may be seen as ways of talking about our lives, ways of
constructing them, living them out and representing them to
ourselves that mask inequitable social arrangements. In other
words, we may be entering into forms of life which are not
necessarily in our own interest, but are in the interests of relatively
powerful groups in society, because the discourses available for
framing our experience obtain our consent; and of course feminists
(though not necessarily calling themselves social constructionists)
were among the first to develop critiques of notions such as
'romantic love'. From a classic Marxist view, marriage and the

family play a crucial role in the maintenance of capitalist economy. It is vital that men, as workers, are able to appear each day in the marketplace ready to sell their labour power. They need to be fed and clothed, to have their health attended to and to be relieved of other family responsibilities like taking children to school or to the dentist and doing the shopping. Women therefore play a central role both in this daily 'reproduction' of the labour force, and in its renewal from generation to generation in the form of children who will in their turn become workers. But it is also vital that women provide these services free of charge. If women did not marry, have children and provide their caring and sexual services free of charge, these things (cooking, laundering, child care and so on) would have to be paid for, via the wage packet, by employers. The idea of the 'family wage' (i.e. that a man should be paid enough money to support not only himself, but a dependent wife and children) serves further to legitimate women's position as provider of free services to their husbands and families. But if you were to ask a selection of men and women why they think people get married and what they think marriage is about, it is unlikely that these ideas would feature in their accounts. The discourse of 'romantic love' serves to re-cast this economic arrangement into a narrative of a mutually beneficial, caring relationship freely entered into for personal, emotional reasons. Men and women get married because they love each other, and women care for their husbands and families because they love them.

In effect we have here two accounts, two different constructions, with conflicting stories to tell about marriage and the family – the 'romantic love/marriage/family' group of discourses and the 'Marxist discourse', and it is the former 'version' of events that is understood as 'common sense'. In Foucault's terms, the power which is exercised through these discourses (in persuading women to give away their services willingly, and in persuading men that the money they receive in their wage packet is a fair exchange for the work they have done) is so successful because of the extent to which it has been possible to obscure its operation by the discourses of love, marriage and family life.

This analysis is reinforced by an examination of the prevailing discourses which construct homosexuality and lesbianism. They are primarily those of unnaturalness, perversion and sickness. At their most charitable, they characterise homosexuals as suffering from an unfortunate illness, for which they are not to blame but for which they ought at least to seek help. At their least charitable, these discourses represent the homosexual or lesbian as morally reprehensible, or even evil. These discourses serve to place homosexual and lesbian relationships outside the orbit of what is considered 'normal' and 'natural' (though by now it should be clear that these terms themselves are not unproblematic) and allow them as only marginal forms of social life with no legitimation. In fact recent legislation such as Section 28 of the Local Government Act in the UK, which makes it illegal for local government funds to be used to 'promote' homosexuality as a 'pretended family relationship', and proposed legislation such as limiting AID (artificial insemination by donor) to married women (it would actually be illegal to discriminate against lesbian couples), are social practices which go hand in hand with and support these discourses. On one edition of the UK Channel 4 programme *Out on Tuesday* (which deals with gay and lesbian issues) Margaret Thatcher, then Prime Minister, spoke out against allowing AID to lesbian couples, again referring to them as 'pretend families'. Why should it be that the images on offer for representing homosexuality are so pejorative? If it is true that the heterosexual nuclear family is the keystone of our present capitalist economy, then homosexuality and lesbianism pose a threat to this status quo. Those who stand to benefit most from society as it is presently arranged have a vested interest in marginalising family forms which appear to question the naturalness and moral righteousness of heterosexual, married family life. This includes single-parent families, and there has recently been fierce political debate in the UK over the payment of benefits to single parents.

In the above examples I have tried to show how prevailing discourses mask the operation of power and are tied to social practices and structures, keeping them in place. However, I do not want to give the impression that discourses and their attendant practices form some kind of impenetrable web, locking us all into our oppression for evermore. At it is sometimes phrased in social constructionist writing, 'Discourses are not monolithic.' They do not interlock neatly with each other, cleanly sealing off all possible cracks and weaknesses. There are weak points, places where they may be attacked, and points at which other discourses pose a real threat. The important point to remember about the nature of discourses is that they are always implicitly being contested by other discourses; this is Foucault's point about power and resistance always operating together. Where there is power there is also resistance. And this is the key to the possibilities for social and personal change to be found within the social constructionist perspective.

Kitzinger (1987, 1989) shows how lesbians whom she interviewed were able to draw upon alternative discourses in forming their own identity as lesbians and in accounting for themselves and their relationships to other people. She shows how they drew upon the discourses of 'romantic love' and of 'self-actualisation' (both of which she identifies as 'liberal humanist' in flavour) in bringing off accounts of themselves which presented them as more similar than different to other ordinary women. She describes the liberal humanistic framework as one which stresses the essential personhood of the lesbian and the relative unimportance of her sexual preference. The lesbian, within liberal humanist discourse, should be accepted as part of the rich variety of humanity.

Liberal humanism could be said to be a heavily legitimated discourse in our present-day society, with the self-contained, free individual at its heart. The discourse of 'the individual' is central to our present social and economic organisation, and as such it is a rich source of material for those who wish to use it to represent themselves in an acceptable way. In other words, calling upon images from the individualist, liberal humanist discourse in order to construct an account of oneself is likely to be quite successful, given the stronghold that this way of viewing human beings currently occupies in contemporary western societies. This discourse presents a picture of the human being in which every person has an equal right to happiness and self-fulfilment. It stresses the person's individuality and uniqueness, and his or her need to make his or her own decisions about how he or she ought to live his or her life. This means resisting the categories and generalities in which society may deal, affirming individuality rather than commonality. Kitzinger (1989) gives some examples from recorded interviews with lesbian women, showing how they used the liberal humanist discourses of 'true love' and 'true happiness': 'I just fell in love with her, and it seemed that if I really loved someone that deeply and that passionately, then nothing we did together could really be wrong' (p. 88), and 'To me, it's been the flowering of my own autonomy and independence . . .

For me being a lesbian really is a positive experience – freedom, happiness, peace with myself, everything!' (p. 91). Kitzinger goes on to suggest that, far from being a step in the right direction, i.e. towards a more humane and accepting view of lesbianism and homosexuality, the use of the 'true love/true happiness' discourses only serves to emphasise their apparent moral rectitude, to entrench them further in our 'common-sense' view of human beings. If it is true that these discourses serve to obscure oppressive relations in society (between workers and employers, between women and men, and between hetero- and homosexuals), then these women are doing nothing to help either the general state of affairs or their own oppression. She concludes with the rather pessimistic view that '. . . the oppressed are actively encouraged to construct identities that reaffirm the basic validity of this dominant moral order' (p. 94).

There are a couple of points that are worth drawing from this. Firstly, it demonstrates the way in which identities are struggled after by people. We are all in the process of claiming and resisting the identities on offer within the various prevailing discourses, and it is when we look at those who appear to be on the margins of mainstream society that we see this struggle writ large. However, Kitzinger's concluding remarks could seem to suggest that no matter how hard you try to 'break out' of the discourses maintaining your relatively powerless position in the world, the whole discourse system closes in around you and you end up caught up in it again sooner or later. I do not think that this is what she is saying, but she does demonstrate that discourses which are threatening to the status quo (and therefore to those who benefit from it), such as political lesbian or radical feminist discourses, which explicitly challenge existing social institutions, will be strongly resisted and marginalised. The process of constructing and negotiating our own identities will therefore often be conflict ridden, as we struggle to claim or resist the images available to us through discourse.

The second point is that power is always relative. It is a mistake to believe that discourses which offer the possibility of a degree of power are reserved for particular individuals or groups. As in the above example, even those in a marginal position can gain some validation by drawing upon suitable discourses. And a single discourse may have complex power implications for those attempting to use it. For example, Hollway (1981, 1984) identifies what she calls the 'male sexual drive discourse'. This is a system of representations of male sexuality, ways of talking and thinking about it, which constitutes the prevailing, common-sense view. It constructs male sexuality as the manifestation of a powerful biological drive. Men are therefore seen as having a basic need for sex which they cannot ignore, and which must be satisfied. It has been commonplace for men who rape to be treated sympathetically by the courts, in recognition of their assumed undeniable sexual requirements. The male sexual drive discourse can therefore be seen as a potential source of power for men, who may sexually assault women with some impugnity or benefit from the controlling effect that the pervasive threat of rape has upon women generally.

However, as I pointed out earlier, power is never a one-way street. The male sexual drive discourse not only constructs male sexuality as driven by a biological imperative, but represents women as potential 'triggers' which can set it in motion. Accordingly, rape victims considered to have dressed 'provocatively' have been seen as bringing on the attack. But this discourse itself thereby endows women with a certain measure of power. Women have the power to elicit men's desire, and are therefore a potential source of danger to men. A man whose sexual drive is awoken may feel himself to be on board a runaway train. His usual sense of self-control may frighteningly evaporate in the presence of an attractive woman, someone who has the power to trigger urgent desires and who also has the power to satisfy him or deny him satisfaction. It may still be the case that this particular discourse affords men more power than women, but the example serves to demonstrate that power is never absolute. It also cautions us against assuming that to have access to power is unproblematically a 'good thing'.

One of the main points of this chapter has been to suggest that discourses can operate to obscure the power relations operating in society. This seems to imply that, by taking on board particular discourses as ways of representing our experience to ourselves, we are living under an illusion. For example, if women marry, have children and look after their families because patriarchal/ capitalist society requires this for its continuation, are they deluding themselves when they say that they married because they were in love and look after their families because they love them? This raises a whole host of difficulties for the social constructionist, which I have already outlined, including the nature of subjectivity, the possibility of human agency, the relationship between discourse and reality, and the concept of truth. I will now go on to discuss these issues in more detail, and to look at how they have been addressed.

SUGGESTED FURTHER READING

Henriques, J., Hollway, W., Urwin, C., Venn, C. and Walkerdine, V. (1984) *Changing the Subject: Psychology, Social Regulation and Subjectivity*, London: Methuen. A 'classic' text in the field, though not an easy book for beginners. The chapters do vary in their accessibility, however. Social constructionist ideas are applied to the areas of work, racism, child psychology, gender and power relations in general. It includes a chapter on the construction of the 'subject' in psychology.

Rose, N. (1989) *Governing the Soul: The Shaping of the Private Self*, London: Routledge. Rose undertakes a Foucauldian-style analysis of our modern concept of selfhood.

Sawicki, J. (1991) *Disciplining Foucault: Feminism, Power and the Body*, London: Routledge. A collection of well-written essays in which Sawicki assesses the strengths and weaknesses of Foucault's ideas. In particular, she applies his concepts of power and resistance to sexuality and mothering, and looks at the usefulness of his approach for feminism.

Chapter 5

Is there a real world outside discourse?

When social constructionists talk of the way in which discourses can be employed to keep people willingly in a condition of oppression, they have sometimes drawn upon the sociological notion of ideology. The concept of ideology is often used by social constructionists to talk about the way in which discourses obscure such power relations. Ideology is a term which can have a variety of meanings, and if it is going to be of any use to social constructionism we need to think about what implications the various meanings have and which is the most useful to social constructionism. I will concentrate here on four understandings of ideology, since they raise important questions for social constructionism, not the least of which is the issue in the title of this chapter.

IDEOLOGY AS FALSE CONSCIOUSNESS

A very widespread understanding is the classic Marxist view. This is the view of ideology as 'false consciousness'. The basic assumption underlying this view is that there is a real, material state of affairs (e.g. that employers pay their employees less than the full value of the work they do, and are thereby able to extract a profit: the real state of affairs is therefore that the workers are exploited), but that people do not recognise (and therefore revolt against) this reality because it is obscured by widely accepted ideas and beliefs. People are thus said to be living in 'false consciousness' because their understanding of their position is distorted. For example, a poor peasant, who is deeply religious and believes that if he works hard and accepts his lowly place in society he will be rewarded in heaven, is suffering, in this view, from false consciousness. Religion here is an ideology in that it keeps him in his place and supports the dominant groups in his society. In so far as the comforts of religion are false comforts, he is alienated from true sources of personal satisfaction. The ideology serves to mask the contradiction in society between the exploitative economic relationships that it involves and the need for some kind of minimum consent from those who are disadvantaged.

Implications for social constructionism

This version of ideology certainly enables us to take a critical stance on the discourses and narratives prevalent in society and ask what effects they are bringing about, but it also brings with it some difficult problems for social constructionism. Firstly, in the example above, the man's religion is 'real' to him and it may well give him 'real' comfort. Similarly, in the example I used earlier, a woman's love for her husband and family and her desire to care for them are equally real and cannot be reduced to illusions or misconceptions. A big problem for Marxist ideology is the image of the person that it necessarily imports; human beings become potentially irrational creatures committed to a way of life which is not in their best interest. How is it possible for people to be self-deceived in this way, and what kind of psychology must we adopt in order to understand this self-deception? It is this problem that has led to the popularity of psychoanalytic theory among Marxists. Psychoanalysis can accommodate false consciousness because it says that the real reasons for people's actions and choices often lie in the unconscious and are not readily available for rational examination. Social constructionism has the same problem; if discourses mask an underlying reality of which people are kept ignorant, what kind of status do individuals' accounts of their feelings, motivations and desires have? This question has not really been adequately answered. As I mentioned in the previous chapter, the explanation that discourses are held to form the conceptual frameworks against which people make sense of their lives and their personal experience is offered as some account of how discourses come to be 'lived out' in the consciousness of us all from day to day. But it says nothing about the psychological processes by which this is achieved; the issues of psychology and subjectivity within a discourse analysis of the person have not been adequately addressed. (In chapters 7, 8 and 9 I will outline the questions about psychology and subjectivity that need answering, and look at some of the approaches that have emerged.) The idea of 'false consciousness' also brings essentialism with it. Clegg (1989), drawing on Laclau (1983), says that the category of false consciousness is tenable only if the person has a fixed, true identity which she or he is capable of recognising.

Clegg goes on to show the implications that this has for the concept of ideology. Rather than ideology being the misrecognition of the person's true interests and true identity, it becomes instead the non-recognition or denial of the person as decentred, fragmentary and unstable. This means that all forms of talk, representation and social practice which insist that human beings have a particular nature (e.g. individuality, femininity, personality and so on) which is somehow inevitable, perhaps 'natural', are ideological.

Secondly, the 'false consciousness' notion of ideology raises the issues of reality, truth and relativism. These are problems which go to the very heart of social constructionism and are not just limited to the question of what we mean by ideology, though they are problematic here too. If we say that people are living in a false consciousness, we are assuming that there is a 'reality' (in which they are oppressed) which lies outside of their understanding of the world, i.e. it is a version of events that is more valid or truthful. This at least involves a value-laden assessment of what is truly in a person's interests, and raises questions about who has the right to make such judgements. But the idea that there is one version of events that is true (making all others false) is also in direct opposition to the central idea of social constructionism, i.e. that there exists no 'truth' but only numerous constructions of the world, and which ones receive the stamp of 'truth' depends upon culturally and historically specific factors. This is what is called 'relativism' – there exist only numerous versions of events, all of which must theoretically be accorded equal status and value. Because there can be no truth, all perspectives must be equally valid. Different viewpoints can therefore only be assessed in relation to each other (hence 'relativism') and not with respect to some ultimate standard or truth. This view is certainly that espoused by Foucault, who insisted that the term 'ideology' assumes that there is a truth, and that we should instead speak of 'regimes of truth', where one regime is no more correct than another. Given that an explicit aim of the social constructionist is to 'deconstruct' the discourses which uphold inequitable power relations and to demonstrate the way in which they obscure these, it is difficult to see how it is possible to do this without falling back upon some notion of 'reality' or 'truth' that the discourses are supposed to obscure.

A further problem such relativism poses regards the status of social constructionist accounts themselves. If all accounts (including scientific and other theories) are equally valid, how can social constructionist accounts justifiably have any special claim to truth? Bury (1986), focussing upon social constructionism in medical sociology, points out that the fundamental problem of relativism in social constructionism has generally not been properly addressed by many writers. Drawing on Gabbay (1982), he points out that the relativism inherent in social constructionism puts its very own premises in doubt, and that the best we can do is perhaps to use the insights offered by social constructionism and put up with the consequences.

IDEOLOGY AS KNOWLEDGE IN THE SERVICE OF POWER

A more useful way of thinking about ideology, for the social constructionist, is to see it as knowledge deployed in the service of power. This view detaches ideology from questions of truth and falsity. A version of events, or a way of representing a state of affairs, may be true or false, but it is only ideological to the extent that it is used by relatively powerful groups in society to sustain their position. Thus ideas in themselves cannot be said to be ideological, only the uses to which they are put. The study of ideology is therefore the study of the ways in which meaning is mobilised in the social world in the interests of powerful groups (Thompson, 1990).

Implications for social constructionism

This view allows us to say that discourses may be used ideologically. The discourses themselves can therefore be said to be neither oppressive nor liberating, and this is a point which

Foucault was at pains to make clear. Foucault held that just about any discourse could theoretically be used to good or bad ends, and that there was no way of predicting the final outcome of the struggles in which discourses may be deployed. Every discourse is potentially dangerous. Bury (1986) gives a good example. Attacks on the medical profession's power to define illness and allocate resources have, in the context of recent political developments in Britain, begun to look rather different. Today the 'New Right' attacks medical autonomy as part of a more general argument for individualism and choice in a view of the health services as consumer goods.The irony is that those 'radicals' calling for alternative medicine find themselves arguing for the self-same values, i.e. consumer choice and free market competition, which underpin contemporary capitalist society.

IDEOLOGY AS LIVED EXPERIENCE

The third view of ideology, which also has something to offer social constructionism, helps us to go beyond the assumption, implicit in the previous two accounts, that ideology is concerned only with what people *think*. The French philosopher Althusser was concerned to stress that ideology is 'lived experience'. Ideology is present therefore in not only what we think, but what we think about, what we feel, how we behave, and the pattern of all our social relationships. Althusser uses the term 'ideological state apparatuses' to refer to the mechanisms by which people are manipulated and controlled by ideology. Schools, the church, the media, the family and so on are all regarded as ideological state apparatuses, and the ideas and ways of thinking that these apparatuses entail cannot be separated from their practices. For example, the ideas of sin, humility, obedience to a higher authority and so on cannot be separated from the practices of going to confession, prayer and kneeling before the altar. Even the structure of the church building itself, which may have, say, a spire 'pointing' to heaven is part of this ideology. So for Althusser, ideologies have a material nature. They comprise a 'package deal' of material things, practices and ideas that are woven into each other. Thus ideas and representations are neither ideal (i.e. existing only in the realm of thought) nor real, for they have no independent existence of their own. An ideology always exists in an apparatus and its practices.

Implications for social constructionism

Although this view has a tendency to see ideology as existing everywhere, which to some extent deprives it of its analytical 'cutting edge' (if everything is ideological, the concept is not much use), Althusser is surely right to widen the scope of the concept to the ways in which ideology pervades everyday life. If, say, British nationality is an ideological matter, it must be reasonable to look at the way we represent Britishness in phenomena as disparate as chocolate boxes with Constable's *Haywain* on the front, Coronation mugs, Kenneth More in the film *Reach for the Sky*, the last night of the Proms and the FA Cup Final. We can therefore think of the ideological workings of discourses as located not only in our language, but also in the social practices in which we engage as a society.

IDEOLOGY AS DILEMMATIC

This view of ideology is in many ways similar to that held by Billig *et al.* (1988). They hold that our thought, its content and processes, are provided by wider, socially shared concepts and issues. The concepts, values and beliefs of the society into which we are born shapes what we will think about, but it also shapes what we see as the two sides of an argument or issue. For example, in our society we might wonder whether traditional or progressive education is better for children, or whether we should blame the poor or the state for poverty. According to Billig *et al.*, thinking itself is characterised by this 'dilemmatic' nature, i.e. it takes the form of a dilemma, a two-sided question to which there is no easy answer. Whatever we are thinking about, it is always, either explicitly or implicitly, part of a two-sided (or many-sided) debate taking place in our thoughts. We therefore think in terms of dilemmas, and what Billig *et al.* call 'ideological dilemmas' simply refer to thinking which is shaped by prevailing ideologies in our society. For example, the ideology of 'the individual' has pervaded our mental life, and in our thinking it is manifested in terms of dilemmas such as whether we should give priority to the freedom of the individual or to the overall good of the collective, i.e. society.

Billig *et al.* see ideologies, like all other ideas, as being themselves inherently dilemmatic. Ideologies cannot therefore be thought of as coherent, unified systems of ideas, but always consist of a dilemmatic opposition, so that the ideology of the individual already contains within it its opposite, i.e. collectivism.

Implications for social constructionism

There are important implications of this idea for social constructionism. It suggests that, although the content of our thoughts is provided by wider social concepts and values, we do not simply absorb them uncomplicatedly and live them out in our lives. First of all, ideologies are not coherent, unified systems anyway, but always (at least) two-sided and as such do not present a 'story' that can be lived out in this way. And second, the nature of human beings is such that our very thinking processes involve us in debate, argument, weighing up pros and cons and so on. In this account, human beings are not like sponges, soaking up ideas from their social environment, but are rhetoricians, arguers, people who are constantly engaged in exploring the contrary implications of ideas. The person here is an active thinker, someone capable of exercising choice and making decisions about the strengths and weaknesses of her or his society's values and ideas.

Taking the useful aspects of all of these views of ideology, then, we can think of discourses as systems of meaning, ways of representing ourselves and our social world, which constitute not only what we think and say, but what we feel and desire and what we do. Discourses can be seen as having the potential to be deployed ideologically, that is, in the service of power and in the interests of the relatively powerful groups in society, but may at the same time allow room for people to exercise some degree of choice in the discourses they take up and use. Science itself, and of course the social sciences such as psychology, have been analysed as an ideology which is constructed through various rhetorical devices and linguistic practices (Billig, 1990; Kitzinger, 1990) and which is used in the services of relatively powerful groups in society (the 'scientific' concepts of 'race' and 'intelligence' are examples).

DISCOURSE AND REALITY

However, although, as we have seen, it is possible to talk about ideology without getting embroiled in the issues of truth and reality, these remain a big problem for social constructionism since, as I pointed out, the absence of an ultimate truth seems to be the foundation upon which the theoretical framework is built. Within this framework it is enormously difficult to say that some ideas or ways of thinking about the world are correct and others false. It is also difficult to conceptualise the relationship between discourse and 'reality'. The extreme relativist position seems to lead to the claim that nothing exists except as it exists in discourse, i.e. the only reality that things have is the reality they are given in the symbolic realm of language. This seems to deny that there is any material base to our lives, and 'things' that have a tremendous effect upon us such as the economy, living conditions or health are reduced to being simply the effects of language.

Parker (1992) has attempted to address this problem in order to arrest the 'slide into relativism' which he feels is encouraged by much discourse theory and poststructuralism. His concern is to come up with some conception of a 'reality outside of the text' that still allows a tenable constuctionist position. He suggests that we think of 'things' (of all kinds, including, say, trees, headaches, water, bad temper, intelligence, etc.) as being endowed with one of three 'object statuses': ontological, epistemological and moral/political.

In the ontological realm (ontology is the study of the nature of things or of existence) are objects which form the material basis for thought – without bodies and brains thought would not be possible, and the physical and organisational properties of our environment give us something to 'think about'. These things, then, are taken by Parker to exist independently of human thought processes and language. However, we cannot ever have direct knowledge of them, even though the things themselves make thought possible, because thought necessarily involves a constructive process, i.e. giving meaning to things. The things we have knowledge of therefore have a different object status – 'epistemological' status (epistemology is the study of the nature of knowledge). Things in the epistemological sphere have 'entered discourse'; they are the things we have given meaning to and talk about. The third realm, that of moral/political object status, is seen as a special category of things that have epistemological status. These are objects such as 'intelligence', 'race' and 'attitudes', and are things that can be 'called into being' through discourse, and thus given a reality which can have real effects upon people (e.g. subject them to discrimination or give them greater educational opportunities). Some of the things that exist in the epistemological realm are therefore representations, or ways of understanding, the things that have ontological status (for example chromosomes and electricity), and some of them are things that have been 'invented' through discourse and have moral/political status (like mental illness and personality). The danger is then that objects having only moral/political status are treated as if they had the same kind of 'reality' as ontological things:

> The epistemological status of things, then, is often contested because such things pretend to represent the real (they derive from objects that really exist) when they actually merely represent items constructed in a political rhetoric (they derive typically from ideological pictures of the real). Take the notion of 'schizophrenia', for example, which has a status as an object of knowledge (epistemological), which is now supposed to rest in chromosome 5 (ontological) but which is actually distilled from debates in medical psychiatry (moral/political).
>
> (Parker, 1992: 31)

Parker goes on to suggest that we should extend the category of 'ontological status' to include all the aspects of our physical and social environment that structure our action. We are born into societies in which life is lived out in a certain kind of physical space (e.g. houses, offices, schools and factories) which are physically and socially organised in ways that impose constraints on what it is possible to do and say:

> In a capitalist economy, for example, industrial workers are physically located for much of the time together with others, and certain types of collective action make sense. In patriarchal societies in the West, women are physically located in homes for much of the time and certain types of collective action do not make sense. In a world organised by structures of imperialism, victims outside and inside the industrial centres can only act, accept or resist, in particular ways.
>
> (Parker, 1992: 36)

This means that if the character of daily life for men is such that they spend much of their time in close physical proximity and are located in the workplace alongside other 'workers' in different accommodation to 'managers', representations and accounts which focus upon 'fraternity' and 'solidarity' may well emerge. These accounts go hand in hand with the action which such arrangements also make possible, such as joining a trade union and going on strike. For women, whose daily lives typically isolate them from each other (or at least do not provide many opportunities for them to come together in large numbers) such accounts and action are unlikely, and some feminists have suggested that the lack of a focus for 'organising' (in the same sense as the trade unions) makes it difficult for women to take collective action to improve their position in the world.

Thus, for Parker, there is a reality that exists outside of discourse, and this reality provides the raw material from which we may structure our understanding of the world, through discourse. This reality consists not only of the physical properties of our bodies and the possibilities and constraints of that bodily life, but also of the properties and organisation of the physical and social environment in which we live.

An important point to emerge from this is the idea that while reality does not determine knowledge, it lays down important restrictions on the variety of ways open to us to 'construct' the world. Barnes (1977) views knowledge as the outcome of people wrestling with, trying to manipulate and trying to control the real world in which they live. Knowledge is found useful precisely because it enables people (to some extent) to manipulate and predict reality. Therefore knowledge must, to that extent, be a function of what is real, and not simply the product of thought, ideas and imagination.

We should perhaps be cautious, however, in accepting Parker's system of categorising things according to their 'object status'. His argument rests upon the idea that things may really belong to one category (the moral/political) and are 'passed off' as belonging to another (ontological) for political ends. This raises, at the very least, the issues of how we are to distinguish the members of one category from another, and who is in a position to make such judgements. Nevertheless, Parker has provided a suggestion as to how we may resolve the problem of the relationship between discourse and reality, an issue which social constructionist writers may well wish to side-step.

At the other end of the spectrum, Edwards *et al.* (forthcoming) explicitly argue that nothing exists beyond the 'text'. We cannot step outside of language and perceive aspects of the world that we have not constructed through it. In line with their general theoretical and methodological approach (which I examine in more detail in chapter 10), they present the relativism/realism debate as one which is worthy of our attention as social constructionists primarily because it is of interest to analyse how these two different accounts of the world are constructed and what rhetorical devices are used to do that constructing.

The issues that I have been dealing with in this and the previous chapter have a direct bearing upon the question of human agency and the possibilities for personal and social change. The major thrust of social constructionism is the claim that human beings, and all the other 'things' consciously present to us, are socially, discursively produced. Some structuralists take the extreme view that people do not speak but rather are 'spoken' by discourses. People thus become the puppets of the ideas they (erroneously) believe to be their own, and their actions are determined by the underlying structure of ideas and language rather than by their own choices and decisions. Are we therefore the unknowing victims of discourses? If this is the case, we should give up trying to get people to change their beliefs or to make different choices, because these things are effects rather than causes of change in the world.

AGENCY AND CHANGE

The question as to whether social constructionism allows us any notion of human agency is again a problem which arises from the fundamental conception of the social world offered by this theoretical framework. If human beings and the things that form the objects of their knowledge are constructed through discourse, then this seems to afford more agency to discourse than it does to people. Certainly, if we are to characterise the experience and behaviour of human beings as nothing more or less than the manifestations of prevailing discourses, then there really does not seem to be much point in suggesting that people can change their situation or that of others by their own intentions and actions. However, this is a very extreme view, and one denied by social constructionists who are concerned with change. Even Foucault, who is often considered to lie at the 'human-beings-as-manifestations-of-discourse' end of the continuum, may have been misrepresented in this respect. It is true that he rejected humanism (the idea that because we experience ourselves as having goals, purposes and intentions we are the sole source and free agents of our actions), but, as Sawicki (1991) points out, this may not necessarily close the door on human agency. She sees Foucault's notion of the person as still allowing for some kind of agency. Although the person, the subject, is constituted by discourse, this subject is yet capable of critical historical reflection and is able to exercise some choice with respect to the discourses and practices that it takes up for its own use.

Within this view, change is possible because human agents are capable (given the right circumstances) of critically analysing the discourses which frame their lives, and of claiming or resisting them according to the effects they wish to bring about. Foucault proposed that change is possible through 'opening up' marginalised and repressed discourses, making them available as alternatives from which we may fashion alternative identities. This is a form of 'consciousness-raising', and the purpose of it is not to impose another, though different, identity upon us (which would be just as oppressive), but simply to free us from our usual ways of understanding ourselves. This view thus sees people as simultaneously constructed by discourse and using it for their own purposes.

The notion of the person as 'discourse-user' has been taken up by Gergen in his idea of 'warranting voice' (Gergen, 1989). According to Gergen, we are all motivated by the desire to have our own version of events prevail against competing notions. We are all competing for 'voice' or the right to be heard, and we therefore present constructions of ourselves that are most likely to 'warrant voice', i.e. to use representations that offer us some validity and legitimacy. In these terms, the lesbians in Kitzinger's (1989) study were 'warranting voice' by speaking through the discourses of true love and true happiness.

Some versions of events 'warrant voice' more than others (i.e. are heard more frequently and are more likely to receive the label of 'truth' or 'common sense'), and this may be because those in relatively powerful positions have both the resources and the authority to make their versions of events 'stick'. For example,

companies may spend huge amounts of money to fill the media
with certain representations of their products, and those in positions of authority such as doctors 'warrant voice' in the sense that
they have the capacity to legitimate their own version of an event
(by making a diagnosis) over that of their patients (who may
have a different story to tell about what is happening to their
bodies). Thus in these examples the ability to bring off an effective construction of events is tied to the power of money and
medical authority. We can therefore say that, in Gergen's terms,
those in relatively powerful positions 'warrant voice' more easily
than others.

In ordinary everyday life too, we are all engaged in this process
with each other, and in this context, with our friends, family and
workmates, 'voice' is determined by how skilful a person is at
using the warranting conventions belonging to her or his particular society. So that an important part of warranting one's actions,
of making them appear reasonable and justifiable, is having the
ability to present oneself in different ways according to the
demands of the moment. Gergen suggests that in our society
there are a number of compelling means of achieving 'warrant',
and in particular he says that referring to mental events as a justification is very common, i.e. people can claim superiority of voice
because they represent themselves as having particular characteristics of mind. He gives an example:

> On the everyday level, for example, one may justifiably make a
> claim to voice on the grounds of possessing privileged mental
> representation or experience. 'I know', it may be ventured,
> 'because I saw it with my own eyes'; 'I heard it'; 'I tasted it'; and
> so on. On the other hand, 'You are ignorant because you have
> no experience.' Or alternatively, one may claim, 'My position is
> based on reason; I am logical while your position is irrational.'
> As a third alternative, 'He should be trusted because he has
> good intentions; I realize his opponents have good arguments
> but I don't trust the intentions behind them.' Fourth, 'True
> understanding comes only from a passionate engagement with
> life; the unfeeling, uncaring, cool and disengaged are some-
> what less than human.' And finally, 'Our common sense of
> morality depends that we take action; failing to do so we are
> morally contemptible.' In each of these cases, then, justification
> for voice rests on the declaration of an allegiance to a different

mental process, entity or characteristic: observation, rationality, intention, passion and moral value.

(Gergen, 1989: 74–75)

Gergen goes on to point out that such warrants are not likely to go unchallenged. If they were to be accepted by others, this would signify that those others had given up *their* claim to voice. Counter-moves are thus made, such as 'You may have seen it, but you had no real comprehension of what you were looking at' or 'The road to hell is paved with good intentions' and so on. What this suggests is that the people who successfully manage to 'warrant voice' do so because they are particularly adept at using these warranting conventions. Therefore people who are skilled 'discourse-users' have at their disposal the means to bring off their desired identity construction for themselves, and to resist those offered by others. Billig's view of the person as 'rhetorician' has similar qualities, focussing upon the ways that people use their capacity for argument, justification, criticism and so on to achieve particular social effects (Billig, 1987). Some social constructionists are quite explicit about how they themselves are using rhetoric and argument to warrant their own, social constructionist, views, and this is part of the 'reflexivity' of the approach (which I will talk about in more detail in chapter 10).

The implications of this view are threefold. Firstly, it gives us an insight into why different people or groups may employ different constructions of events, and why the same people may use different constructions of the same event on different occasions. Constructions arise not from people attempting to communicate supposed internal states (such as feelings, desires, attitudes, beliefs and so on which emanate from their 'personality') but from their attempts to bring off a representation of themselves or the world that has a liberating, legitimating or otherwise positive effect for them. This would include the tendency for those in positions of power to legitimate and endorse constructions or discourses which maintain and justify that position. Secondly, it suggests that the agency of human beings lies in their ability to manipulate discourse and use it for their own ends. This puts the person firmly in the driving seat, and implies that personal change is at least a possibility. By challenging and resisting the representations of ourselves on offer in prevailing discourses, we have the chance to construct or claim alternative identities for ourselves. And thirdly, it implies that this ability is in the nature of a skill, and therefore, in principle at least, could be improved, thereby increasing the agency of the individual.

This view of the person as 'discourse-user' is therefore a facilitating one. It holds out the possibility of change through personal agency and choice. However, it could be seen as paying insufficient attention to the ways in which the claim to 'voice' are constrained. We do not all have equal 'access' to all discourses. Our class, age, gender, ethnic origin and so on all impose restrictions upon the kind of person we can claim to be, and this is surely not best understood as the operation of individual differences in a skill. Nevertheless, it does draw attention to the 'performative' aspects of language, i.e. the way in which language is used to do things, to bring about effects in the world, and is an accessible way of conceptualising the human being as agent. It also has practical advantages, in that it offers some kind of implicit recommendation as to what a person might actually do to claim legitimation for a particular representation of themselves or of others. I have used Gergen's notion of 'warranting voice' to illustrate the view of the person as a user and manipulator of discourses, and not simply a product *of* them. But this is not the only 'discourse-user' account, and I shall look at other models in chapter 7.

The problems of agency, relativism, reality and truth are difficult ones indeed for social constructionism, and their complexity is reflected in the way that they are often written about in the literature. These are perhaps the most confusing and conceptually difficult areas in social constructionism, and my aim here has been simply to outline why they are problems and to introduce some of the (limited) ways they have been addressed. One of the ways of getting away from the idealism of the theory (idealism is a philosophical position which claims that it is only *ideas* of things, and not things themselves, which can be said to exist) is to say that discourses, social structures and social practices are intimately bound up with one another. This at least seems to accord as much importance to material reality as to the ideas and discourses supporting that reality. However, social constructionism is still open to a further criticism, i.e. that it is a 'top-down' theory in disguise. 'Top-down' in this context means that the flow of influence or determination travels from society down to the individual, so that individuals are seen as the products or outcomes of the society in which they live. If a discourse analysis of individuals and their social world can be reduced to a 'top-down' theory, then it is redundant because it has nothing useful to add to existing analyses. It is to this problem that I now turn.

ACKNOWLEDGEMENT

I am indebted to Dallas Cliff for material used in this chapter.

SUGGESTED FURTHER READING

Billig, M., Condor, S., Edwards, D., Gane, M., Middleton, D. and Radley, A. (1988) *Ideological Dilemmas: A Social Psychology of Everyday Thinking*, London: Sage. A well-written and entertaining book, putting forward the authors' view of the dilemmatic nature of thought and a model of the person as 'rhetorician'.

Parker, I. (1992) *Discourse Dynamics: Critical Analysis for Social and Individual Psychology*, London: Routledge. A major concern of this book is the relationship between discourse and reality.

Shotter, J. (1993) *Cultural Politics of Everyday Life*, Buckingham: Open University Press. In this book, Shotter develops his idea of conversation as the primary human reality, a view which he shares with Harré.

Chapter 6

Can individuals change society?

In the last chapter, I ended by addressing the issue of personal agency, and asked how, within a social constructionist framework, individuals could be thought of as being capable of changing themselves or their social environment. I showed that this is a problem for social constructionism because of its view of the person as the product of discourse. However, there is another source of difficulty regarding human agency which faces the social constructionist, and this is the relationship between the individual, society and discourse.

In several places I have talked about the way in which discourses, social practices and social structures are bound up with one another, so that they form a coherent package. At the same time, it has also been suggested that the social environment we live in, how our living and working arrangements and our time are structured, provides a material basis from which some representations or discourses rather than others seem favoured to rise to prominence. If we give due credit to the power of social structure to influence the lives of individuals and the discourses that are available to them, do we have to say therefore that individuals and the discourses with which they frame their lives are the products of social structure? This is an important question, because if the discourses through which people experience their lives and their world are themselves the products of social structures, then to bring about any changes in the world we must target those structures and not the discourses they produce. This would be a typical structuralist view of the world, and an understanding of discourse or psychology would become redundant. Within this view, it is once again difficult to conceptualise individuals as having basic human agency, as having the capacity, through their own actions, to change the face of the society in which they live. It also questions whether there is any point in trying to address inequalities by resisting prevailing discourses or otherwise trying to change the language we use.

THE AGENCY/STRUCTURE DEBATE

This debate is one which has continually dogged the social sciences. The problem of how to understand the relationship between the individual and society has revolved around the issue of the direction of influence: do individuals determine society (i.e. bottom-up), or does society determine individuals (top-down)? If individuals logically pre-exist society (i.e. if society arises from and is based upon the nature of the individual), then the notion of human agency is preserved. Society becomes the product of all the individual choices and decisions that people have made, and what we call 'society' amounts to little more than the sum total of all the individuals living in it (this is referred to as 'methodological individualism'). But it is hard to explain why the nature of human beings appears to change according to the kind of society in which they live, and to account for the orderliness of society. Why should millions of individuals independently choose to get married, have children, decorate their houses in similar ways or wear similar kinds of clothes? If society is seen as determining individuals, this problem is answered but in the process we lose human agency; it can be no more than an illusion or misconception. Individuals become the products of the kind of society they are born into, and their choices and decisions are explicable in terms of societal norms and values.

In fact, both top-down and bottom-up conceptions of the relationship between the individual and society are problematic for social constructionism. The top-down view leaves discourse as a side-effect of social structure, and it therefore cannot be the focus for social change. The bottom-up view, worse still, cannot accommodate any kind of social constructionism, since the individual is taken to be logically prior to the social. The individual is a 'given' from which society arises, and which therefore cannot be said to be constructed by that society. This methodological individualist view has all the attributes fiercely contested by social constructionists. It is humanistic and essentialist, claiming for the human being an essential nature, a coherent, unified self, and the capacity to make self-originated choices and decisions.

In this chapter I will focus primarily upon this 'bottom-up' view, because it forms the foundation of traditional psychology, as well as our common-sense understanding of the world. Good accounts of 'top-down' sociological views are given by Frisby and Sayer (1986), Craib (1992) and Giddens (1984).

THE BOTTOM-UP VIEW OF THE WORLD

The view of the individual as a pre-given entity from which society, as a secondary phenomenon, arises is at the heart of the discipline of psychology. The whole enterprise of psychology, which aims to explain and predict human experience and behaviour, is therefore, from the social constructionist perspective, based on false premises. It is at best misguided, since it does not address itself to the real sources of personhood, and at worst oppressive, since its practices and knowledges serve to uphold inequitable power relationships in society.

Before going on to look at how the individual/society problem might be resolved satisfactorily for social constructionists, it is worth spending some time expanding upon traditional psychology's view of the individual and how the person's social environment has been treated. An important issue for psychologists arises here. If psychology has misconceived the nature of human beings, then there are two possibilities for the future. One is that psychology is irrelevant and redundant because the reasons for people's behaviour and experience are not to be found inside their heads. The other is that we need to develop a different kind of psychology which can accommodate and complement social constructionist accounts of the person. This is an issue that I will take up in the next three chapters.

The individual and the social in psychology

The traditional psychology and social psychology that we are familiar with today have their roots in the experimental laboratories of the North American universities, and are therefore often referred to as 'North American psychology'. Historically, they have operated upon the assumption that the behaviour and experience of human beings can be understood by looking for intra-psychic explanations, that is, by looking for structures and processes operating within the 'psyche' of the individual person. Many of the topics of central concern to psychology have been those that we ourselves feel to be located at the level of the individual, such as memory, perception, motivation, emotion and so on. It seems to us that our memories, our feelings, drives, etc., are private events (private in the sense of originating within us and being available only to us inside our own heads). Traditional psychology rests upon this assumption, and has taken the behaviour and experience of this self-contained individual as its standard. Within this view, 'pure' measures of things like memory capacity, perceptual accuracy and personality traits can theoretically be obtained by filtering out as many variables as possible that might influence the person.

The psychological laboratory epitomises the search for the ideal environment where all such variables could be either eliminated or controlled. The aim here is therefore to remove the person from her or his usual environment, where there are too many contaminating variables to obtain a pure measure of the person's 'real' nature. For example, in order to assess the effects of alcohol upon mood, it would be necessary to isolate the experimental subject from possible distorting influences such as the presence and behaviour of other people, the light and heat conditions of the room, its decoration and so on.

Thus the normal social context of the person's everyday life is seen as full of variables which distort and disguise the individual's capacities and characteristics. When they *are* studied, social factors are manipulated experimentally in order to assess their impact upon behaviour. The nature of 'the social', therefore, within this view, is an array of variables which can distort, mask, exaggerate or otherwise modify the basic capacities and character of the individual. A good example of this is the traditional conception of attitudes (e.g. Fishbein and Azjen, 1975; Azjen and Fishbein, 1980). Here, 'attitudes' refer to the way we feel about something, whether we are 'pro' or 'anti', have positive or negative feelings about it. Although there is a common-sense assumption that we behave in accordance with our attitudes (for example, a person who holds 'right-wing' attitudes might be expected to behave accordingly by voting Conservative in an election), there is much evidence to suggest that this is very often not the case (see Wicker, 1969, for a literature review). However, the response of attitude theory to this problem has been to suggest that there are a great number of variables external to the individual, such as the norms and values of their society, how their action would make them look to other people, the consequences of their action and so on, that modify the expression of the person's basic attitude.

When psychologists first addressed phenomena that were less obviously intra-psychic, such as prejudice and racial discrimination, it was with the assumption that they could be explained by looking inside the minds of individuals. Complex social phenomena were seen as reducible to the thoughts, feelings and motivations of individual actors. For example, Allport (1924) accounted for racial disharmony by suggesting that it arose from the basic inferiority of black people's personalities. Today this would certainly strike us as a racist view, and we would at least want to bring into the equation such factors as bad housing, poor job prospects and inequality in education. However, this example is only an historical and extreme form of psychology's general tendency to explain social phenomena by appealing to intra-psychic events and processes. Later, Adorno *et al.* (1950), trying to understand the origins of the strong anti-Semitism of Nazi Germany, suggested that it lay not in the personality of the victims but in that of the anti-Semites. Adorno postulated that prejudice arose from having an 'authoritarian personality', which in turn came from having been brought up by very strict parents who meted out harsh discipline. This is a more liberal view than that of Allport, but nevertheless it still attempts to explain prejudice in terms of intra-psychic processes.

The present discipline of social psychology grew out of concern with such pressing social issues, and the questions surrounding the formation of attitudes and their susceptibility to change have for decades been at its centre. However, despite social psychology's concern with explicitly social problems, these were at first conceptualised as explicable in terms of individual psychology. In fact, Allport (1924) explicitly gives this as his objective, believing that interactions between individuals must ultimately be explained in terms of intra-psychic events.

The idea that the phenomena of social psychology could be understood as the product of *social* factors impacting upon a pre-existing individual began to appear in psychology a few decades ago, and was present in introductory psychology texts such as Hilgard *et al.* (1971), who state that the social context of individual behaviour is always an influence upon it. Although this was a step in the right direction, in that psychologists were beginning to realise that adequate explanations of human behaviour had to take into account the social context in which people live, it still gave that context only secondary status in the sense that it was seen as something 'added on' to the individual. This is demonstrated by some of the classic social psychological research carried out in North America. For example, in the 'conformity' research of Asch (e.g. Asch, 1956), individuals were asked to make a number of perceptual judgements. In one condition, subjects were asked to make their judgements alone, and accuracy rates in this condition were very high. In a second condition, individuals gave their judgements after a number of other subjects (who were in fact confederates of the experimenter) had given their, erroneous, judgements. In this condition, the 'naive' subjects agreed with the confederates in about one third of the trials. In these trials, the subjects are said to have 'conformed' to the apparent group norm set up by the confederate subjects. This study implies that individuals when on their own are able to make rational, reasonable judgements, but that when in a group they become affected by extraneous factors, such as reluctance to 'rock the boat', desire to feel part of the group and fear that others will reject or dislike them. The rational individual is portrayed as undermined by the features of the group. In a similar vein, the 'bystander apathy' research (e.g. Latané and Darley, 1970) showed that individuals on their own were more likely to come to the aid of someone in distress, or to report an emergency, than if they were in a group. Explanations such as 'diffusion of responsibility' suggest that individuals' natural sense of responsibility becomes eroded when they are in a group with others. The implication of both these studies is that individuals are somehow changed by the presence of their fellow human beings, and that this is a change for the worse. It appears that the usual rationality and morality of the individual are undermined by their presence in a group.

Now I do not wish to criticise such research, in the sense of suggesting that it was conducted badly or that the results were misinterpreted. However, it is always true that the answers you get depend upon the questions you ask. If you begin with assumptions about the pre-given nature of the individual, you will limit yourself to answers that are framed in terms of the effects that social factors can have upon that nature. The outcome is less likely to be interpretable in terms of the mutual interdependence of the individual and the group, or the ways that groups may be influenced by individuals. Although Moscovici *et al.* (1969) did demonstrate that a consistent minority can substantially influence majority opinion, the greater part of research in social influence has documented the dangers to individual reason and morality present in group processes.

There are two points to note about this. One is that such research necessarily leads in the direction of a particular view of humankind. The results apparently leave us with questions like 'Why has responsibility for action been diffused?' and 'Why do people ignore the evidence of their own eyes?' The only way we can make sense of this is to see people as having a kind of 'blind spot' where others are concerned. Human nature is such, it would seem, that ordinary, reasonable, rational, moral individuals are susceptible to outside influence and should be on their guard against this 'contamination'.

The second point follows from this. If we step back from this research and look at it within the historical and social context in which it takes place, it is possible to see that it is based upon and perpetuates the individualism of western capitalist society. We are invited to place value upon the lone, self-contained individual who is capable of making his or her own decisions regardless of the opinions of others, a person whose sense of morality is firmly located within his or her own mind and is not susceptible to outside influence, a person whose sense of himself or herself comes from an internally located, stable and integrated identity, and who does not have to fall back upon the regard of the group for his or her self-esteem. This is the picture of the isolated, self-sufficient individual that I described earlier as neatly serving the purpose of our current economic and social structure. Conversely, an image of the person as primarily part of a larger functioning unit (the group or society) gives primacy to the identity of the collectivity rather than the individual, and stresses commonality of purpose rather than individual difference. To stress such commonality of interest and purpose is a short step from a society based on communist rather than capitalist principles, and one where collective action might seem more likely than inter-individual competition.

Let me sum up the points I have so far been trying to make here. If we look at the classic research of both psychology and social psychology, we can see that it is intrinsically individualistic, according prime importance to intra-psychic events in the understanding of both individual behaviour and experience and social phenomena. This in itself makes psychology and social constructionism uneasy bedfellows. Furthermore, not only are social factors seen as simply another set of variables which can influence the individual, but such influences are perceived as likely to be dangerous.

The problems with individualism

Thus we can see psychology and social psychology, rather than as value-free, as operating within a value system which is historically and culturally specific. In a sense, what I have said here therefore amounts to a social constructionist analysis of psychology. This is not to say that psychologists have deliberately 'fudged' their data in order to make certain interpretations more likely, but that psychologists, like all other scientists, are also human beings and like everyone else they are located inside a value system from which their questions about the world arise. Furthermore, the individualism of psychology can have other effects which are worrying for social constructionists. Going back to the example of theories of prejudice, explanations which locate the problem either within the personality of the victim or within that of the prejudiced draw attention away from prejudice and discrimination as widespread societal phenomena, and away from the power relations which are often fundamental to them. To describe prejudice against black people as an idiosyncratic personality deficit draws attention away from the fact of the social and economic inequalities that exist between black people and white people, and how these inequalities are maintained through social institutions such as education and the law. Similarly, to look at sex discrimination as if it were the effect of some individuals holding inappropriate attitudes is to divert attention from the way that women are systematically marginalised in politics, the law, education, industry and commerce; in fact in every sphere of life where influential decisions are taken by powerful people.

Such conceptualisations in the end do not explain things very well. Attitudes towards women have received much attention, and attempts have been made to change the way people think about men and women; revisions of children's reading schemes,

TV programmes about masculinity and new images of women and men in TV advertisements, newspaper articles and so on, not to mention innumerable discussions, arguments, negotiations and rows enacted between countless individual women and men throughout society. Yet despite this, the inequalities between the sexes have not greatly lessened. What has psychology to say about this? Simply that attitudes are so 'entrenched' that they are slow to change. And yet, to use a metaphor like 'entrenched', though it conjures up images of the battlefields of the First World War and invites us to visualise those attitudes deep in the dug-outs of our minds, refusing to give up the fight, does not explain anything. By what psychological process does an attitude become 'entrenched'? What does it mean to say that an attitude is 'entrenched'? That it is resistant to change? If so, why does it have such resistance, when other attitudes (for example, attitudes to clothes, wildlife, child rearing) are changed quite rapidly relative to the human lifespan? Psychology draws a blank here, and it is only when we move away from an individualistic framework that we can offer some answer to these questions (for example, change is slow to happen because it is in men's interests to resist it, and they do so through their control over the major institutions of society). These answers are certainly contestible, but at least they are compatible with the evidence. What psychology tends to do, then, is to de-politicise social problems by locating them at the level of the individual psyche, and this is another reason why social constructionism and psychology presently do not mix. One of the explicit aims of much social constructionist research is to analyse the power relations within which people live their lives (including the power of psychology as a field of scientific 'knowledge', as discussed earlier) and thus within which their experience is framed, and to offer an analysis which allows the person to facilitate change.

My aim here has not been to subject traditional psychology to a thorough critique, but to show the nature of some of the differences between it and social constructionism. In particular, it has been to show the limitations and dangers, from a social constructionist perspective, of such a 'bottom-up' view of the relationship between the individual and society.

We can see that there are two possible models of this relationship within traditional psychology and social psychology. One is that there are basically only individuals, and that all other phenomena (like society) are 'side-effects' of the nature of the individual. In this view, individuals create or at least influence society. The second possibility is that social arrangements (e.g. groups, communities, societies) can have an effect upon the individual. Although the flow of influence is in the opposite direction, this view still has at its heart the autonomous, pre-existent individual that is already there, ready to receive social influence. Writing about psychology's conception of the relationship between individuals and others, Sampson says:

> The conformity tradition in the American version of social psychology, for example, stands as clear testimony to the manner by which we both understand personhood and cherish independence ... We pay lip service to interdependence, but invariably insist that the parties to this interdependence must first clearly and firmly define themselves independently ... I previously referred to this version of personhood by the term self-contained individualism ... This describes a character whose clear boundaries separate self from other, and who is thereby able to function independently.
>
> (Sampson, 1990: 118)

'Top-down' views, which see individuals as products of social structure, only differ here in terms of the direction of the flow of influence. Both are problematic for social constructionism, for the reasons outlined earlier.

The problem seems to lie in the way that the individual and society are seen as the two components of a dichotomy. In the real world, we never actually see 'society' on the one hand and 'individuals' on the other. It is not like looking at an egg and a hot frying pan and asking what effects each has on the other (the frying pan hardens the egg, and the egg makes the frying pan eggy). One solution to the individual/society problem is therefore to suggest that this is a false dichotomy, a division that is an artefact of intellectual analysis by human minds and not a division that represents discrete phenomena. In other words, the individual/society dichotomy can be thought of as a construction, one way of thinking about the world, but not necessarily a way we have to be committed to.

AN ALTERNATIVE TO THE INDIVIDUAL/SOCIETY DICHOTOMY

Of course, simply pointing this out does not make it any easier to envisage an alternative. The dichotomy of individual/society, like those of mind/body, reason/feeling and free will/determinism, is so fundamental to our way of thinking that imagining alternatives is like imagining what might lie outside the universe. Sampson (1989), drawing upon the French philosopher Derrida (1974, 1978, 1981), suggests that this is because these dichotomies arise from a general feature of thinking in western societies that has been with us for thousands of years. I will spend some time now outlining the relevant features of Derrida's argument, so that we can see how it may be used to solve the individual/society problem.

Derrida and deconstruction

Derrida's ideas are not especially easy to understand, so let us build up the argument by going back to an issue that I talked about in an earlier chapter; the relationship between the signifier and the signified. Saussure had claimed that, though this relationship was arbitrary, the signifier (for example, the word 'tree') and that which it signifies, its meaning (our idea of a tree), are bound together. The meaning becomes 'fixed' to the signified. The word 'tree' therefore has attached to it all the 'treeness' qualities we think of when we think of the real object (leafy, tall, shady and so on). But Derrida, as part of the growing poststructuralist movement, questioned the idea that meaning could ever be present in the signifier in this way. Poststructuralism points out that the meaning of signifiers (such as words) is constantly changing, is context-dependent and not fixed. Words mean different things in different circumstances, depending upon who is using them, when, on what occasion, and upon the context of the rest of their talk. Even within a single sentence, the meaning of one word can only be determined retrospectively, as later words form the context for it.

But more than this, Derrida sees language as a self-referent system. Signifiers in the end can only refer to other signifiers. Sarup explains it like this:

> Suppose you want to know the meaning of a signifier, you can look it up in the dictionary; but all you will find will be yet more signifiers, whose signifieds you can in turn look up, and so on. The process is not only infinite but somehow circular: signifiers keep transforming into signifieds, and vice versa, and you never arrive at a final signified which is not a signifier in itself.
>
> (Sarup, 1988: 35)

Thus signifiers, such as words, only gain their meaning from other signifieds. It is the word's relationship to other words which gives it its meaning. The meaning of, say, the word 'darkness' only emerges through its relationship to other words such as 'light'. In fact, just as we might think of darkness as being the absence of light, Derrida suggests that all signifiers are like this; the identity of something is given by that which it is not, that which is absent from it. The meaning of 'tree' is therefore to be found in all the things that are absent from it. 'Tree' is *not* shrub, *not* flower, *not* animal and so on. But of course we are not conscious of this when we use words, and mistakenly believe that the meaning of a word is fully present in that word alone. Thus, for Derrida, meaning is always both dependent upon a signifier's difference from other signifiers and constantly deferred from one signifier to another in an endless chain. Derrida uses the French term '*différance*' to refer to these features of difference and deferral.

When we talk about something, whether it be society, minds, freedom, or dogs and cats, we are therefore always implicitly also referring to what these things are not, to what is absent from them. These absences are repressed; we forget they are there, and Derrida suggests that we need a way of revealing their action in our language. His methodology for achieving this is called 'deconstruction', and involves very closely reading a piece of text with an eye to showing up how its construction relies upon such unstated absences.

I will say more about deconstruction later, when I talk about the analysis of discourse for research purposes, but for the moment the important implications of Derrida's ideas lie in the nature of identity. The identity of any object of our consciousness, be it tree, dog, table, love, freedom or darkness, lies not simply in that object itself but also in all the things it is not, in absence as well as presence. To give anything an identity, to say what it is, is necessarily also to say what it is not. In this sense, presence contains absence. That is, to say that a quality is present depends upon implying what is also absent. If we apply this idea to the realm of the individual, then it follows that the nature and identity of what is meant by 'the individual' are a function both of itself and of what it is not. Now, if we take the individual/society dualism, this means that the phenomenon we think of as the individual is necessarily defined by its opposite term, not-individual, societal. The nature of things lies in the relations between them rather than in the things themselves:

> As we have seen, Derrida argues that in whatever we take to be immediate and present there is always already absence, difference and deferral. If presence always contains absence, there cannot be a neatly drawn line of opposition between these two notions. It is not that presence and absence are opposites, not that there is either presence or absence, but rather that there is an inevitable defining of the one through the other: there is both presence and absence.
>
> (Sampson, 1989: 12)

If it is not possible to draw a line dividing absence from presence, the same applies to all other oppositions we think with, including mind/body, freedom/determinism, health/illness, masculine/feminine, rational/emotional and so on, and of course individual/society. Derrida's argument is that for thousands of years western thought has been founded upon the logic of such 'binary oppositions', the logic of 'either/or'. Do we have free will *or* are we determined? Are we individuals *or* the product of society? Do we act through reason *or* through our emotions?

Derrida argues that such binary oppositions, in which one term is always given a more privileged position than its opposite, are typical of ideologies. They 'con' the reader into believing in the existence of greater value on one side of the dichotomy rather than the other, when in fact neither can exist without its other. Thus we are led to think of the individual as primary and society as secondary, to think of the mind as superior to the body, and to value reason above emotion. Derrida recommends that we reject this logic of 'either/or', of binary oppositions, and adopt instead a logic of 'both/and'. When considering any phenomenon, in order to understand it properly we should take as our unit of study both what it is taken to be and what it appears to exclude.

Thus, rather than think of the individual and society as forming opposite sides of a dichotomy, we should instead think of them as inseparable components of a system, neither of which can make sense without the other. The individual/society system is therefore the unit of study, as neither term refers to something which, of itself, can be properly understood.

Such a 'deconstruction' can be applied to other problematic dichotomies, such as agency/structure, freedom/determinism and self/other. The questions that these dichotomies pose, such as 'Do we have free will, or is our behaviour determined?' and 'Do we have agency, or are we the product of society?', lose their meaning within this framework. They become inappropriate questions to ask. The importance of dissolving these dichotomies, for social constructionism, lies in the possibility of human agency and the re-conceptualisation of the nature of the individual that they bring with them. If agency and structure are part of one inseparable system, then the effectiveness of human agency is just as real as the determining features of social structure. Of course, just what 'human agency' can now be taken to mean is unclear. It cannot remain the same phenomenon as it appears to be if we think of human beings as uncomplicatedly producing social structure out of their freely chosen actions. This remains one of the many problems for social constructionism that come about when you start radically re-conceptualising fundamental ideas; the nature of everything else has to be re-conceptualised too.

Individual/society as an ecosystem

Let us now look at one possible model for understanding the relationship between the individual and society, and the nature of individuals that it imports, which is suggested by this 'both/and' logic, the logic of supplement rather than contrast. Drawing on Bateson (1972), Sampson (1989) argues that the unit of natural survival is neither the individual nor society. In fact there can be no such 'unit', only a *system*, which Bateson calls the 'ecosystem'. This system comprises both the organism and its environment, both the individual and its society. Sampson therefore invites us to view the relationship between the individual and society as an ecosystem. The study of animals, of the effects of one species upon another and the effects of environment upon species, has not been well served by conceptualising each species as discrete from others, and the 'environment' as some extraneous set of factors which have an 'effect' upon a species. Such ways of thinking encouraged the use of chemicals in agriculture to control pests and diseases without any understanding of the ways that the existence of different species were closely interwoven with each other and with their habitat. Each species forms part of the 'environment' for the other, each producing 'habitats' by the subtle action and interaction of their behaviours. Thus it makes little sense to separate out 'species' from 'environment'; they must be considered as a single system. Sampson recommends that we view the individual and society as such an ecosystem. However, as with the problem of agency, just what this system now looks like, how we describe it and the mechanisms and processes through which it operates, are not clear. All we can say is that these things are likely to be quite different from their nature under the old, dichotomous view.

But this does not mean that we necessarily have to reject all concepts of the individual. After all, we occupy discrete bodies; physically, we are not part of one functioning whole, as are the organs of the body. But persons and bodies are not identical and we need a way of acknowledging the way that self and other are, within a 'both/and' logic, mutually defined. For example, Chodorow (1978) and Gilligan (1982), writing within a psychoanalytic framework about the differences between women's and men's sense of self, suggest that the predominant western notion of the highly individuated, self-sufficient, separate person describes primarily the experience of men. They argue that women's sense of self is that of the 'self-in-relationship', that women's identity is so closely bound up in their relations with others that for them the dividing line between self and other is less clear than for men. The suggestion here is that the person's identity lies in their relation to others, and is not an entity to be found inside the person.

Chodorow makes the point, in sympathy with arguments I outlined earlier, that this sense of self, this version of the individual, arises from women's experience of society and social life, which she argues is typically quite different from that of men. Men primarily inhabit the public world, the world of work, of competition, a world where their skills and talents are pitted against those of their competitors, and these conditions give rise to the 'individual' of western capitalist society. Women's daily experience, typically centred on family life, is lived out in a network of interconnected relationships based not upon competition but upon mutual care and co-operation. Thus the sense of self we come to live out is intimately connected to the kinds of social condition in which we are embedded.

Sampson, focussing upon the increasing 'globalisation' of the modern social world, takes up the theme of the 'embedded' individual as his recommendation for the future welfare of human beings:

> An individualism that derives from this kind of connectedness not only differs from self-contained individualism, but also introduces an alternative principle on which to found the social order.
>
> To be an individual by virtue of one's connections and interconnections introduces a constitutive view of the person that I believe can more adequately include the possibility of human welfare than the current self-contained formulation allows. The embedded or constitutive kind of individuality does not build upon firm boundaries that mark territories separating self and other, nor does it abandon the connectedness that constitutes the person in the first place . . .
>
> Embedded individuality requires a constitutive view of the person, re-embedding free-standing modern individuals in their social worlds and thereby emphasising ensembles of relationships and communities of belongingness rather than isolated nomads. Furthermore, the reformulation is a perfect example of seeking to use our discipline in order to constitute a different kind of social reality. But, I persist in believing . . . that an embedded individuality is not designed with current conceptions of societal management in mind; rather, it responds to a different kind of historical urgency.
>
> (Sampson, 1990: 124)

Discourse and society

If we take up the suggestion that the individual and society, rather than existing as separate but related entities, are part of a single system, then the problems of human agency and the status of discourse are somewhat ameliorated. Individuals, the social practices in which they engage, the social structure within which they live and the discourses which frame their thought and experience become aspects of a single phenomenon. This means that discourses are neither simply a product or side-effect of social structure nor one of individuals. They are embedded in that structure and are part of it, and at the same time serve to structure our identity and personal experience. Thus discourse can be seen as a valid focus for forces of social and personal change.

THE CHALLENGE TO PERSONHOOD

Throughout this book, I have been describing the social constructionist challenge to our common-sense understanding of the person, and to that of traditional psychology. I have thrown into question such notions as the individual and personality, and described radical re-conceptualisations of our notions of language, power and personal identity. All of these issues have major implications for what it means to be a person. Clearly, much of what traditional psychology and social psychology describe as human nature cannot be accommodated within a social constructionist framework. We need to come up with some alternative accounts of personhood that can take its place; in other words, we have to re-write psychology if we believe that the study of individuals still has a place. Most social constructionist accounts are counter-intuitive; they appear to be telling us that what we had previously felt to be self-evident about human beings, that the very terms in which we experience our selves and our lives, are misleading. At least for this reason, I believe that we are obliged to build some account of our personal experience that, while being compatible with social constructionism, does not reduce that experience to the level of illusion. Clearly, such a model of personhood will have to be radically different from what we are accustomed to, and the theories upon which social constructionism draws do not readily lend themselves to analysis at the level of individuals. So building up such a new picture means coming up with new concepts and applying old ones in different ways.

By questioning the old assumptions of essentialism and humanism, social constructionist theory has moved the centre of attention out of the person and into the social realm. Psychology, within this framework, becomes the study of a socially constructed being, the product of historically and culturally specific discourses,

discourses which bring with them a complex network of power relations. It embeds the person in a historical, social and political fabric from which it cannot be teased out and studied independently.

If we are going to throw out our old descriptions and explanatory devices such as the unified personality, attitudes, traits and so on, how are we to describe the person instead? Are there any characteristics of human beings that can be said to qualify as some kind of 'human nature'? If people experience themselves as having personalities, emotions, drives and so on, how does social constructionism re-conceptualise these phenomena?

These are questions to which social constructionism has largely not addressed itself, primarily, I believe, because these were not the questions it set out to raise (although some interesting work has been done regarding the social construction of emotions; see Harré, 1986a). However, although describing the psychology of the socially constructed person has not been an aim of social constructionist writers, it is possible to begin to build up an image of this person by looking at some of the implications of social constructionist writing.

In the next three chapters, I will examine some of the attempts to re-conceptualise the person, and will try to show what they achieve as well as what they fail to explain. This will involve drawing upon a number of different 'versions' of social constructionism and examining the implications for personhood of what they have to say.

SUGGESTED FURTHER READING

Parker, I. and Shotter, J. (eds) (1990) *Deconstructing Social Psychology*, London and New York: Routledge. This book includes excellent contributions from Sampson, Billig, Kitzinger, Shotter and Rose, among others. It focusses upon a critique of individualism in social psychology, the social construction (and deconstruction) of social science, and issues of subjectivity and individuality.

Chapter 7

What does it mean to be a person?

I The person as discourse-user

The view of people as users and manipulators of language and discourse for their own purposes is one I have outlined earlier, and I will discuss it in more detail here. This is now a position adopted by a number of social psychologists working in discourse analysis but is perhaps most closely identified with Potter and Wetherell's (1987) book. In this chapter I will examine their approach and look at the implications for personhood that it holds.

One of Potter and Wetherell's main concerns was to raise a question mark over the traditional concept of 'attitudes' by subjecting it to a social constuctionist analysis. When social scientists interview a person about an issue, say unemployment, immigration or the health service, they commonly assume that the replies the person gives to their questions are in some way a representation of something that lies inside that person's head, i.e. her or his attitude or opinion on that issue. The language that the person uses, the account that she or he gives, is taken to express unproblematically the attitude that lies within. Potter and Wetherell argue that 'attitudes' in this sense do not exist, and that we only have to look at the degree of variation to be found within any respondent's interview transcript for the proof of this. An 'attitude' refers to a coherent and relatively long-lived orientation to an issue or object, and therefore we should expect that when a person is questioned about his or her attitudes there will be a high degree of coherence and stability in what he or she says. However, Potter and Wetherell show that this is usually not the case. Using their own transcripts from two interview studies, one concerning race relations in New Zealand and the other about the handling of a riot by police, they point out that variability within accounts is the rule rather than the exception. In other words, at various points in the interview, depending upon what question the interviewer was currently asking, respondents would typically give accounts that appeared to be quite incompatible with each other if considered as manifestations of the same underlying attitude. An example of such variation is given in Wetherell and Potter, from interviews about race relations in New Zealand. They give the following quotations from their interview transcripts:

> 'I do this bible class at the moment, not highly religious, I just think children ought to know about religion . . . and last night we were just discussing one of the commandments, love your neighbour, and I had this child who said "What would happen if you got a whole load of Maoris living next door to you?" and I said to him "That's a very racist remark and I don't like it", and he shut up in about five seconds and went quite red in the face, and I realized afterwards that obviously it wasn't his fault he was, turned out to be thinking like that, it came directly from his parents.' . . .

> 'The ridiculous thing is that, if you really want to be nasty about it, and go back, um, the Europeans really did take over New Zealand shore, and I mean that Maoris killed off the Maorioris beforehand, I mean it wasn't exactly their land to start with, I mean it's a bit ridiculous. I think we bend over backwards a bit too much.'
>
> (Wetherell and Potter, 1987: 174, 175)

Both extracts come from the same interview, i.e. from a single respondent, and Wetherell and Potter argue that it would be impossible from this to determine the person's 'attitude' towards the Maoris. Could this person be described as 'tolerant' or 'prejudiced'? Would she or he be in favour of or against multiculturalism? The 'attitude' displayed here is neither coherent nor stable. Wetherell and Potter suggest that, rather than take what people say as an expression of internal states or underlying processes we should look at what people are doing with their talk, what purposes their accounts are achieving. And since a person may be trying to bring about different effects with his or her talk at different points in the interview, it is not surprising that we find the variation that we do. This view therefore denies that there are any internal structures to the person that we could call 'attitudes' and instead looks at what people say as intentional, socially directed behaviour which performs certain functions for them.

THE PERFORMATIVE VIEW OF LANGUAGE

Our talk has specific functions and achieves purposes for us in our interactions with each other, and being interviewed by a social scientist is just a particular form of social interaction. The approach builds upon the earlier traditions of 'speech act' theory and ethnomethodology. Speech act theory, usually associated with the philosopher Austin, was an attempt to get away from the idea that the prime function of language is to describe some state of affairs, some aspect of reality. Austin (1962) pointed out that some sentences or utterances are important not because they describe things but because of what they do, and Potter and Wetherell give some examples:

For instance, the sentence:

I declare war on the Philippines

is not a description of the world which can be seen as true or false but an act with practical consequences; when uttered in the right circumstances it brings into being a state of war. Austin called sentences of this kind performatives. Other examples are:

I name this ship the Lady Penelope

Beware of the bull

I sentence you to six months hard labour

In each of these cases, the primary role of the sentence is not description as such but to make certain things happen; they are sentences performing acts.

(Potter and Wetherell, 1987: 13)

Speech act theory therefore draws attention to language as a human social practice. This view of language as functional rather than descriptive is also common to the sociological tradition of ethnomethodology. The word 'ethnomethodology' simply means the study of the methods (methodology) used by the people (ethno). It is the study of the methods that ordinary people use to produce and make sense of everyday life. Again, rather than view the things that people say as simple descriptions of reality, ethnomethodologists look at the functions that people's talk has within an interaction and the effects it achieves for them. Both for speech act theory and for ethnomethodology the things that people say become the object of study themselves rather than being taken as a route to discovering some aspect of an assumed underlying reality, like a person's attitudes or the causes of a particular event. (For a brief account of the links between speech act theory and ethnomethodology see Potter and Wetherell (1987), chapter 1.)

This approach to talk gives rise to a number of questions which are very different from those of traditional psychology. It leads us to ask what functions people's talk might have for them, what purposes they are trying to achieve, and what linguistic devices they employ to bring about the desired effects. It encourages us to catalogue the range of linguistic devices and rhetorical skills that are brought into play for specific purposes and to ask by what methods people construct their talk to achieve the effects they do. These are the questions addressed by Potter and Wetherell and by others working within this version of discourse analysis. Let us now take a look at some of the possible answers to these questions that have emerged from research studies in order to gain a better picture of the model of the person that is implied here.

INTERPRETATIVE REPERTOIRES

The person as tool-user

Potter and Wetherell (1987) put forward the concept of the interpretative repertoire as a way of understanding the linguistic devices that people draw upon in constructing their accounts of events. Interpretative repertoires can be seen as:

> the building blocks speakers use for constructing versions of actions, cognitive processes and other phenomena. Any particular repertoire is constituted out of a restricted range of terms used in a specific stylistic and grammatical fashion. Commonly these terms are derived from one or more key metaphors and the presence of a repertoire will often be signalled by certain tropes or figures of speech.
>
> (Wetherell and Potter, 1988: 172)

Thus, interpretative repertoires can be seen as a kind of tool-kit of resources for people to use for their own purposes. They represent a consistency in accounts which is not located at the level of the individual speaker. That is, although an individual may display a high degree of variability and inconsistency in her or his account of a single event or object, nevertheless we all draw upon the same tools in the tool-bag from time to time. Identifying an interpretative repertoire is rather like an archaeologist inferring the past existence of a particular type of widely used chisel or spear by observing a number of different instances in which it appears to leave characteristic, tell-tale traces.

The functions that these repertoires serve for people are seen as generally enabling them to justify particular versions of events, to excuse or validate their own behaviour, to fend off criticism or otherwise allow them to maintain a credible stance in an interaction. Some examples of research using interpretative repertoires will illustrate this.

Potter and Reicher (1987) analysed the way that the terms 'community' and 'community relations' were used in different accounts of the 'St Paul's riot' of 1980. This was a period of some hours when fighting took place between police and youths in the St Paul's area of Bristol. Potter and Reicher subsequently analysed a number of accounts from local and national newspapers, television reports and records of parliamentary proceedings as well as transcripts of interviews with some of those involved in the incident. They found that 'community' was repeatedly used in connection with phrases and figures of speech from three basic metaphors: a spatial one (for example, the phrase 'close-knit'), an organic one (talking of 'growth') and agency (speaking of the community as taking action). Furthermore, it was universally used to carry a positive meaning and value; 'community' was seen as a good thing. However, different accounts, coming from different sources, used the 'community' repertoire to accomplish different effects. For example, in some instances the riot was characterised as a problem of 'community relations'. Within these accounts, the police were represented as forming a part of a wider community which was suffering from difficulties in interpersonal relations and trust. Other accounts, by contrast, used the 'community' repertoire to characterise the event as an open conflict between the 'black community' on the one hand and the police on the other. By using the repertoire in these contrasting ways, those giving the accounts could 'warrant' different versions of the event, motivations could be ascribed to participants and blame apportioned, as well as solutions to the problem put forward. Potter and Collie (1989) suggest that the 'community' repertoire is also brought into use in a quite different context, that of 'community care' for the mentally handicapped. The use of the 'community' repertoire in this context, they suggest, can be used to represent the closure of mental hospitals as somehow a cosy and neighbourly solution to a financial problem.

Thus, the 'community' repertoire can be seen as a collection of metaphors and linguistic devices which could be drawn upon by virtually anyone in order to bring about a particular, desired representation of an event. Repertoires, then, do not belong to individual people and are not located inside their heads. They are a social resource, being available to all who share a language and a culture, and are seen as a tool-kit from which people can assemble accounts for their own purposes. The person in this model is an active participant in social life, busily engaged in constructing accounts for various purposes, but without (apparently) any psychic content such as attitudes, ideas and motivations. Potter and Wetherell go to great lengths to eschew any cognitivist feel to the idea of interpretative repertoires (i.e. the idea that repertoires are inside people's heads and direct their behaviour), but it is hard to consider the question of why accounts might be constructed in one way rather than another without recourse to some kind of internal explanation, such as belief or motivation. Potter and Wetherell are not primarily interested in issues of personhood, and therefore these matters are not addressed by them. But we are left without any clue as to 'who' is doing the constructing and why.

The person as moral actor

Wetherell and Potter (1988) identify three of the repertoires used by interview respondents in their study of racism in New Zealand. The 'culture-fostering' repertoire presents the view that Maori culture should be encouraged and protected both for the sake of its uniqueness and distinctiveness and in order to provide Maori people with a sense of their own historical and cultural roots. A second repertoire, that of 'pragmatic realism', stressed the promotion of things that are useful and relevant to modern-day life, and the third repertoire, 'togetherness', advocates the view that there should be no divisions or barriers between people; we should all see and treat each other simply as people, regardless of colour or cultural background. Wetherell and Potter suggest that these repertoires are used by their respondents to create accounts which relieve them of a moral responsibility for action and which effectively justify and validate the status quo. The 'culture-fostering' repertoire is based upon the notion that Maoris lack something that ought to be regained; they are deficient culturally. What function does this serve for respondents?

> Firstly, it seems to make sense of another commonplace under-standing that Maoris have a deprived social position and are discontented, through using the idea of rootlessness and loss of identity. In this lay sociology, people without roots – those who have 'lost' their identity in some way – do not perform well and are likely to agitate. Secondly, in using the notion of cultural deficit speakers can effectively place Maori problems elsewhere, removed from their own responsibilities and actions. In this way speakers can convey that they themselves are in no way to blame for these problems ... Respondents virtually never characterized the inclusion of Maori culture in a way which involved active effort or change on their own part; effort and change was depicted as a Maori problem and duty.

> (Wetherell and Potter, 1988: 179)

Although often used by the same respondents who drew on the cultural-fostering repertoire, the 'pragmatic realism' reper-toire seems radically different. It embodies the idea that, on simple practical grounds, nothing can be gained from trying to encourage Maori culture because it simply is not relevant to modern-day life. Maori cultural practices are represented as unrealistic or impractical; they are old-fashioned and should be abandoned. Wetherell and Potter suggest that the repertoire of pragmatic realism is a particularly flexible one, and it enables speakers to paint a picture of constraining factors which may be regrettable but which are nevertheless beyond their control. They can thus at the same time represent themselves as people who are realistic and practical.

The 'togetherness' repertoire, in the context of national unity in New Zealand, was seen as being used to imply that Maoris should stop encouraging conflict between them and (white) New Zealanders, while maintaining a 'caring' gloss on the account.

This is typical of much interpretative repertoires research, in that the respondents can be seen to be concerned to position themselves acceptably with respect to the moral rules and expectations of their culture. The person is therefore located as an actor or performer in a moral sphere, a person whose prime aim in constructing her or his account is to construct herself or himself and her or his actions as morally justifiable.

Let us now summarise the model of the person that this approach appears to assume. Firstly, it imbues the person with agency, since the construction of accounts is achieved by people choosing and implementing forms of representation appropriate to their immediate goals. The person is therefore actively engaged in the process of construction, building up an account of an event from the linguistic materials available in interpretative repertoires. Active selection is implied, since the person has to choose the appropriate devices for the task in hand out of the many available linguistic resources. Some writers, such as Billig (1987, 1991) have focussed upon researching in detail the way that accounts are organised, using particular rhetorical devices, to achieve their effects.

Secondly, it sees people as primarily located within a local moral order within which they have to negotiate a viable position for themselves. The functions which their constructed accounts serve for them are primarily those of offering explanations and excuses, making justifications, apportioning blame and making accusations. People are therefore actors in a moral universe, concerned with negotiating for themselves a credible (and creditable) moral position.

In many ways, this view is similar to that of Gergen (1989), outlined earlier, who sees people as motivated by a desire for 'speaking rights' or 'voice', and to have their interpretation of events accepted as the truthful one. The person who is able to 'warrant voice' is therefore a skilled operator with a good understanding of warranting conventions. But in order to warrant one's actions, to give a socially acceptable account of them according to context, it is also necessary to draw upon a variety of different representations of selfhood. For example, versions of selfhood or human nature could include 'people as unique collections of traits', 'people as bearers of original sin', or 'people as basically all the same underneath the skin'. Such accounts of selfhood could be used, say, to justify competition, to advocate some form of social control, or to gain support for a multicultural initiative. Gergen implies that these different versions of selfhood have emerged as people throughout history have found it necessary to construct and elaborate them into an armoury with which to fight their own personal or group battles for 'voice'.

This view suggests that the prime motivation in social interaction is to gain voice, which of course will have a diversity of practical, social consequences. Those who are able to warrant voice are likely to enjoy greater power in society, may be given greater resources (money, jobs education, etc.) and will enjoy generally higher social standing. Gergen seems to see the individual's motivation to acquire 'voice' as the source of the variety of representations or discourses of selfhood that are currently available. However, Potter and Wetherell (1987) draw back from such an individualistic account. Although they themselves are primarily interested in the ways that individuals construct accounts for their own purposes, they also recognise (in common with poststucturalist writers in the Foucauldian tradition) the way that linguistic practices are tied in with particular forms of society and social practice.

Unintended consequences of accounts

Although Potter and Wetherell recognise that the implications of what people say, the repertoires that they draw upon, go beyond the immediate social situation they are engaged in, they emphasise that such implications and consequences may be unintended by the speakers themselves. They make a clear distinction between the person's reasons for using particular discursive forms and their social psychological consequences. When people speak, they may not be aware of the associations and implications that their choice of words brings with it. Furthermore, people's use of interpretative repertoires and their efforts to construct events in a particular way may be conducted at a non-conscious, non-intentional level. When people use repertoires, they are not necessarily acting in a machiavellian fashion, but just simply doing 'what seems appropriate' or 'what comes naturally' in that situation.

Language and subjectivity

Although not primarily concerned with the nature of selfhood implied by their account, Potter and Wetherell do occasionally go beyond the performative aspects of language to glimpse the relationship between language and subjectivity. By way of an illustrative example, they describe selfhood from the perspective of a culture very different from that of western industrialised societies, that of the Maori. Drawing upon Harré (1983) and Smith (1981) they describe what appears to constitute person-hood for the Maori. For the Maori, the person is invested with a particular kind of power, called 'mana', which is given to the person by the gods in accordance with his or her family status and birth circumstances. This mana is what enables the person to be effective, whether in battle or in everyday dealings with others. This power, however, is not a stable resource, but can be enhanced or diminished by the person's day-to-day conduct. For example, someone's power could be reduced if he or she forgot one of the ritual observances or committed some misdemeanour. People's social standing, their successes and failures and so on, are seen as dependent upon external forces, not internal states (such as their personality or level of motivation). Potter and Wetherell suggest that people living in such a culture, holding such beliefs, would necessarily experience themselves in quite a different way from that which we are used to:

> If one views the world in this kind of way, with the individual seen as the site of varied and variable external forces (and mana is only one of these possible forces which inhabit the indi-vidual), then different kinds of self-experience become possible. Specifically, individuals can cease to represent themselves as the centre and origin of their actions, a conception which has been taken to be vital to Western concepts of the self. The indi-vidual Maori does not own experiences such as the emotions of fear, anger, love, grief; rather they are visitations governed by the unseen world of powers and forces, just as an inanimate object, a stone or pebble, can be invested with magical taboo powers so that touching it places the offender in danger.
>
> (Potter and Wetherell, 1987: 105)

They therefore suggest that the very experience of being a person, the kind of mental life one can experience, perhaps even how we experience sensory information, are dependent upon the particular representations of selfhood, the particular ways of accounting for ourselves, that are available to us in our culture.

Potter and Wetherell's account may in some ways appear akin to behaviourism in its view of the human subject. Attention is focussed on what the person is doing (i.e. with their talk), and mediating mentalistic states such as attitudes, cognitions and traits are rejected. However, the person is in no way simply the product of her or his environment, and acts by making (albeit non-conscious) choices from the interpretative repertoires available. The only psychological processes that might be involved appear to be the desire or motivation to warrant voice or to negotiate a viable moral position , although terms such as 'desire' and 'motivation' are conspicuously absent from Potter and Wetherell's book. In common with other social constructionists, they want to remove phenomena that are normally thought of as intra-psychic events from inside the person's head and place them instead in the social, interpersonal realm. However, we are left without any notion of who it is that is doing the constructing, and by what processes. The person is effectively empty, or at the very least Potter and Wetherell are not concerned with the possible content. The subjective experience of personhood is notionally understood to be dependent upon the interpretative repertoires culturally available to us, although again it is unclear how this happens.

Potter and Wetherell therefore use 'interpretative repertoires' where other writers (e.g. Parker, 1992; Hollway, 1984) have talked of 'discourses'. However, although there is enough overlap between the two terms for them often to be used interchangeably, there is an important reason why researchers may wish to distinguish between them (as Potter and Wetherell do). I will talk about the implications of this distinction in a later chapter, when I look at the practice of discourse analysis and what is meant by this term.

SUGGESTED FURTHER READING

Potter, J. and Wetherell, M. (1987) *Discourse and Social Psychology: Beyond Attitudes and Behaviour*, London: Sage. Now a 'classic' text. It gives a clear outline of what the authors mean by 'discourse' and 'interpretative repertoires', with good illustrative examples from research studies.

Wetherell, M. and Potter, J. (1988) 'Discourse analysis and the identification of interpretative repertoires', in C. Antaki (ed.) *Analysing Everyday Explanation: A Casebook of Methods*, London: Sage. A good chapter, introducing the idea of interpretative repertoires.

Chapter 8

What does it mean to be a person?

II The self as constructed in language

Potter and Wetherell have little explicitly to say about the experience of personhood. However, some social constructionists have directly addressed this issue and have attempted to demonstrate how human subjectivity is rooted in the linguistic forms culturally available to us. In this chapter, I will describe two approaches which have a quite different focus from each other, but which are linked in that they try to show how our sense of ourselves as people has its basis in our use of language. The first approach I will describe is that of Harré, who sees our subjectivity as residing in the internal logic or grammar of language. The second approach is represented by Sarbin and by K.J. and M.M. Gergen, and sees our sense of personal history and identity as arising out of culturally available narrative forms.

HARRÉ AND THE GRAMMATICAL SELF

In their description of the Maori self, Potter and Wetherell (1987) suggest that the kinds of way we have available for talking about ourselves give rise to our experience of ourselves as human beings. For the Maori, accounting for oneself in terms of external forces such as *mana* means that all mental life and subjective experience will be 'read off' from this framework. Harré expresses this point well: 'To be a self is not to be a certain kind of being, but to be in possession of a certain kind of theory' (1985: 262).

Harré (e.g. 1983, 1989), drawing upon the philosophy of Wittgenstein and Kant, suggests that our understanding and experience of ourselves as human subjects, our subjective experience of selfhood, is laid down by the beliefs about being a person that are implicit in our language. For Harré, the structure of the language we are born into determines the kinds of belief about personhood that we acquire. 'Beliefs' here do not necessarily mean an articulated set of opinions, but refer to the fundamental structuring of our thinking that is achieved by our use of language. In other words, the structure of our language decrees (or at least very strongly suggests) that we adopt particular fundamental assumptions (i.e. beliefs) about human nature, and live them out in our daily interactions with each other. As an illustrative example, and one which Harré sees as crucial to many of our self-understandings in western cultures, let us look at the words we use for referring to ourselves.

We often use words to refer to the objects around us; we point to an animal and say 'There's a lion', and we make requests such as 'Please pass the brown sauce.' In these cases, the words 'lion' and 'brown sauce' have what Harré calls an 'indexical' function; they 'point to' or refer to existing objects. The words are labels for things. However, he says that we make a fundamental error when we assume that other, more 'psychological' words such as 'I' and 'me' are indexical in the same way. It is as if we (non-consciously) reason that since the words 'I' and 'me' exist, then specific entities referred to by those terms must also exist; there must be an 'I' and a 'me' in the same sense as there are lions and brown sauce. He believes that our language, which has the personal pronoun 'I' (many languages do not use words such as 'I', 'she', 'they' and so on to accompany their verbs), misleads us into this fundamental but erroneous belief. The simple existence of the word 'I' allows us to foster the belief that we are autonomous individuals, that each of us is represented by a coherent, unified self, and furthermore that this self contains mechanisms and processes (the subject matter of psychology) that are responsible for our actions.

Implications of the language of selfhood

The fact that we have two words to refer to ourselves, 'I' and 'me', brings further complications. It gives us numerous possibilities for representing ourselves as divided or conflict-ridden. It is easy to think of 'I' as the authentic, private self who can monitor 'me', a more superficial, social self. We can even postulate the existence of a number of different social selves, and begin to search (as humanist psychologies often do) for the real, authentic self that lies deep within the person. We can think of ourselves as split into conscious and unconscious selves, and contemplate the battle between them, the outcome of which is our behaviour. These ways of thinking, says Harré, are only made possible by the particular grammatical forms present in our language, and we should beware of assuming that real entities such as the self, the ego, the mind, the unconscious and so on exist as objects simply because we have words which refer to them. The concepts for these things certainly exist (and they may have very real effects), but the things themselves do not exist as observable entities in the world.

> We have to immunize ourselves against the reification of beliefs once again . . . Because it [language] is our medium for being as persons, there has been a tendency to take as meta-physical and/or empirical matters that are in a broad sense grammatical – for instance the self, agency, intention and so on.
>
> (Harré, 1989: 23–24)

By 'grammatical', Harré means more than the rules that language-users follow when they make up sentences. I believe that he intends it to have a broader reference, but one which includes this common-sense understanding of the term. The grammar of a language here refers also to the unspoken and largely unarticu-lated rules that people follow in accounting for themselves and their actions. For example, Harré suggests that the language of western industrialised societies is dominated by the logic of exhortation and choice. Our ways of accounting appear to draw heavily upon the exhortation of others or of ourselves and upon the making of (and therefore taking responsibility for) choices. The grammar or internal logic of our language-use therefore refers to the (culturally and historically specific) rules or tradi-tions that people appear to follow when they construct accounts.

The 'splitting' that the words 'I' and 'me' allow can further be used by speakers in a variety of ways for the purpose of giving accounts of themselves and their conduct. In examples such as 'You are not being honest with yourself' and 'Pull yourself together', two different kinds of self are implicitly offered in each statement: the self that is honest versus the self that does not want to face facts, and the strong self that can take control of the weaker self. As well as leading us further down the road of reifying such entities, these linguistic devices are useful tools of self-accounting. 'I couldn't help myself' is a way of disowning responsibility, 'I took myself in hand' a way of claiming credit and so on.

Instead of looking at the words 'I' and 'me' as if they represented real entities, and then going on (as psychologists have traditionally done) to ask questions about the nature of those entities, Harré instead argues that we make use of such words in conversation to perform actions in a moral universe. Harré's position is in this way similar to that of Potter and Wetherell, in that the person as social actor is seen as primarily struggling to represent herself or himself in an acceptable way with respect to their culture's local moral rules:

> Looking still more closely at our conversation shows the enquirer that I, and in other languages the first-person inflection, is used to perform a moral act, an act of commitment to the content of the utterance in the appropriate moral universe ... The human individual is, above all, in those societies that recognize autonomy, a moral phenomenon ... 'I' is a word having a role in conversation, a role that is not referential, nor is the conversation in which it dominates typically descriptive fact-stating. It is a form of life, a moral community that has been presupposed by the uses of the first person, not a kind of hidden inner cognitive engine.
>
> (Harré, 1989: 26)

So here again Harré is stressing the active, performative role that language has, and sees the goal of such performances to be primarily one of accounting for our conduct within a moral framework, i.e. within the specific system of rules of conduct of one's local culture. ('Local', in this context, could, for example, mean western industrialised society, the culture of a particular nation, or a group subculture. It simply refers to the sets of rules and conventions about right and wrong and correct behaviour within which the person is currently operating.)

Harré is emphatic that people are users of rules (moral rules, or the local conventions for accounting for oneself). But rules do not have some independent and concrete existence inside the person; there are no 'rule-following' mechanisms or processes within the mind which determine behaviour. Harré, like other social constructionists, eschews any notion of intra-psychic states and processes such as skills, dispositions, drives, cognitive structures and so on. People learn their culture's rules as they grow up and gradually become adept at their use. The process of psychological development implied by this is remarkably different from those that psychologists are used to. For example, Piaget (1952) sees the child as developing more and more sophisticated cognitive structures with which to apprehend the world, and these are manifested in a series of intellectual stages through which the child passes en route to adult intelligence. The process of development implied by Harré, by contrast, consists not in the transformation of internal structures, but in the gradual acquisition of accounting skills. Development is therefore a process of becoming more and more sophisticated in one's ability to manufacture accounts by using the linguistic and accounting rules of one's culture. Harré sees this ability as developing, at least in part, through the social interactions that take place between infants and their caretakers. Adults interact with and talk to babies *as if* they had desires, intentions, wishes and so on, so that infants, as they also develop language, gradually come to structure their own experience in these terms too (see Harré, 1986b, for a fuller account of his ideas on development.)

This puts the emphasis firmly on the social and linguistic practices embedded in a culture. Harré suggests that this is where psychologists should look if they want to understand human beings. For him, to understand human beings is to understand how different forms of accounting are used in different circumstances, how these forms of accounting are tied in with the grammar of one's language, and how these grammars and accounting practices differ between cultures. In this sense, Harré is quite an extreme social constructionist. For him, there are only two realms of things that make up a human being; there is physiology, and there are linguistic practices. And furthermore, the role given to physiology by Harré does not appear to be very great. For example, we may want to argue that there are some aspects of our psychology which can be said to be non-linguistic and which are closely tied up with our physiology, such as 'skills'. Surely it is not unreasonable to believe that, say, laying a stone wall can be entirely and adequately described by a series of physiological events? However, Harré points out that when we begin to look at any skill, such as playing the piano or carving wood, we are immediately back in the social, linguistic realm. To demonstrate a skill means to have performed in accordance with some culturally and historically specific definition, and to have had one's efforts accounted for in skill-type language. We can begin to see that thinking of even simple 'skills' as the straight-forward manifestation of physiological events is very shaky. We are immediately drawn into issues about who decides what constitutes a skill, how it is deemed to have been performed, and under what circumstances claims to skilful performance are accepted or rejected. Thus, for Harré, the phenomena of human life can very largely be described by linguistic practices. However, Harré does not disregard the self as a psychological phenomenon. He merely denies that it can have any essential, pre-linguistic existence which then causes or determines our experience. He therefore goes beyond Potter and Wetherell's account, since he does specifically address the issues of person-hood and subjectivity.

The language of the self as an organising principle

As human beings, Harré sees us as predisposed to organise our experience in some way, to make sense of it, to pull it together within a framework. Not to do so would result in chaotic, mean-ingless experience, and our concept of selfhood is the result of this structuring. However, the nature of selfhood, the particular kind of structuring we adopt, is culturally and linguistically specific. It is governed by the grammar, or logic, of the language we are born into and acquire. Harré suggests that our 'self' concepts perform a similar function to other concepts we use to organise our experience of the world. He gives the example of the concept of 'gravity' as an illustration.

The concept of 'gravity' gives us a way of organising and struc-turing our experience of, say, falling apples, hot-air balloons and earth satellites into one coherent framework. It gives us a way of classifying different experiential events under the same rubric, and gives us a framework for understanding and making sense of that experience. Harré points out that the power of 'gravity' as a conceptual framework does not depend on our being able to demonstrate whether, in some objective sense, gravity is 'real', i.e. has some ontological reality. Even if 'gravity' is merely a convenient fiction, it still allows us a powerful way of structuring and understanding our world. The same is true, he says, of concepts regarding the self. He suggests that when we use the word 'I' we are referring to a hypothetical entity (the self) in much the same way as physicists are referring to gravity when they use the term 'g'.

The conception of selfhood that we acquire comes from the grammar, logic or underlying metaphors present in our language. Harré sees the job of psychology as one of exposing this grammar and showing how it produces the self as we know it. For example, he notes that many of our accounting processes draw upon a metaphor of 'opposing forces'. We talk of inner conflicts, resisting or giving in to temptation, being steadfast in the face of strong opposition and so on. These ways of accounting, in their turn, are dependent upon a language which is well endowed with the rhetoric of persuasion and command; much of the way we talk about ourselves and others is in terms of persuasion, command, exhortation, influence and so on. These metaphors (e.g. thinking of ourselves as if we were the site of a battle between conflicting forces) form part of our concepts of agency and action, and therefore structure how we account for ourselves. By uncovering the internal logic of language in this way, Harré believes we will be able to understand where our concept of the self comes from.

The human subject described here is a being who learns the socially acceptable ways of accounting for oneself and who learns to become adept at the practice of these, and uses them for his or her own purposes. The human subject is therefore trainable in linguistic practices, but is also liable to be misled by those practices into thinking that grammatical devices, such as the self, have onto-logical status, i.e. that they have some existence outside of language and texts. The experience of selfhood that we acquire as we develop language represents our structuring of experience. This structuring is made possible by the particular internal logic, underlying categories, metaphors and so on of the language we use. We should therefore expect people of all cultures and soci-eties to organise their personal experience into a meaningful system which can be called the 'self', but we should not expect this selfhood to be similar cross-culturally, and the differences between two cultures' versions of selfhood will be rooted in the underlying grammar or logic of their languages. However, it is unclear from Harré's account just what kind of research programme he would advocate in order to study the relationship between language and selfhood, and what kind of data would serve as evidence.

Agency and the grammatical self

Can this human subject, then, be said to be an agent, to 'have' agency? In response to this question, Harré directs us once more to the linguistic practices in which our entire psychology is embedded. Two points are worth making here. Firstly, the history of western thinking has long been rooted in the notion of cause and effect. Causality as a notion has served us reasonably well when it comes to explanations of the physical world. We say that metal fatigue caused a bridge to collapse, or that a series of events inside the engine of a car causes its forward motion. However, when it comes to our own psychology and conduct we have, it is argued, inappropriately imported the logic of cause and effect into our explanations. When we talk about the reasons why we did something, we are misled by our cause–effect thinking into believing that we have uncovered the causes of our behaviour. We are thus led into the quagmire of the agency–determinist debate: are we free to act as we please (within physical and social constraints) or is our conduct determined by (caused by) forces beyond our knowledge and control? Harré argues that when we give reasons for our actions we should not be misled into thinking that we are describing the causes for our behaviour; rather we are providing a narrative account which will succeed or fail according to the local accounting and warranting conventions of our culture. When we hear someone give their reasons for her or his conduct we are therefore witness to an account in the process of construction, not a description of a cause–effect relationship. (Of course, a person may account for his or her action by representing it in cause–effect terms, thereby absolving himself or herself of responsibility for it.) Harré says that we find ourselves in the conundrum of agency (do we have it or not?) because we have confused the 'grammar' of causality with that of authorization. We are simultaneously trying to talk in two different languages, each with its own internal logic, which do not map on to each other.

Secondly, Harré points out that the whole agency debate may only be of importance to people who live in a culture which has been influenced by the Judaeo-Christian tradition, with its emphasis upon personal choice. The Bible is full of stories in which people are faced with choices, between spirituality and materiality, between God and earthly ties, between temptation and resistance, between the easy and the difficult path. We can begin to see that the language of choice, of free will, of personal weakness or strength, of determination and so on, is a language of an historically and culturally specific location. Harré points out that the issue of agency and choice may not be a feature of other cultures and religions; for example, in Islamic cultures the focus is upon how people may bring themselves to act in accordance with choices and decisions that have already been made for them by Allah.

According to Harré, then, once one begins to focus on the conditions of use of agentic-type talk, one begins to see the concept of agency as something which is a product of particular grammatical and linguistic conventions, a notion employed in the accounting devices of peoples of the Judaeo-Christian tradition, and certainly not something which we should think of as a transcendental 'given' of human beings. The question as to whether or not human beings have agency thus becomes a pointless one to ask. Harré asks only how the language of agency is employed in accounts of conduct. He therefore does not primarily concern himself with the issue of agency, and suggests that our problem with it has arisen from asking the wrong question about it, i.e. 'Do we have agency?' rather than 'How do we use the language of agency and to what purposes?' Convincing though this argument may be, the reader may be forgiven for suspecting that an important issue has been side-stepped. What we call 'agency' may well be nothing more than an illusion of language, but we are still left pondering the problem of the extent to which, and by what means, individual human beings are capable of directing and changing their lives and their society.

For Harré, then, the form of subjectivity we live out and experience depends upon the particular theories or 'stories' about the nature of humanity that are to be found embedded in our language. He suggests that our psychology is structured by these things, not by the intra-psychic forms of traditional psychology, such as schemas, dispositions and so on, and encourages us to look to our accounts of ourselves and each other for clues to the 'theories' we are operating.

The idea that human beings strive to organise and make sense of their experience is one shared by other writers too, sometimes coming from very different backgrounds. Kelly (1955), the founder of Personal Construct Psychology, saw this as a fundamental feature of humanity, and the school of *Gestalt* psychology recognised human beings' predisposition to see pattern in their experience. However, three writers in particular are of interest to us here, Sarbin and K.J. and M.M. Gergen, as they propose that the self-in-language is given shape and form by our fundamental predisposition to think in terms of stories or narrative.

THE SELF IN NARRATIVE

Sarbin (1986) argues that human beings impose a structure on their experience, and that this structure is present both in our accounts of ourselves and our experience that we give to others, and in how we represent those things to ourselves. This structure is a narrative structure; we organise our experience in terms of stories. This is in no way to suggest that people are living in a fantasy world or that the stories that people produce are in some way whimsical. Just as Harré sees the structuring of our experience and our self-understandings to be given by the internal logic or grammar of our language, Sarbin suggests that this structuring takes a particular form, the narrative form, and that this is ubiquitous throughout human cultures. He sees it as a fundamental 'given' of what it means to be human.

Sarbin sees narrative, as the organising principle of our psychology, to be present in all manner of facets of daily life. It is present in our dreams and daydreams, in our rememberings, in our plans for the future or for the day ahead, and in our accounts that we tell to others. When we 'remember' a dream, we do not recount a list of unconnected events and images; we see it and recount it as a story that has a beginning, a middle and an end. In some cases, we are aware of having to do a good deal of 'story construction' with the dream material in order to give it a sense of narrative. Even quite abstract and, on the surface, meaningless perceptual events tend to be given narrative structure by people. Heider and Simmel (1944) and Michotte (1963) both report experimental studies in which observers were asked to report what they saw after watching a film of moving geometric shapes. Their reports typically took the form of stories, in which the shapes were cast as human actors engaged in some endeavour.

When we tell someone the story of our life so far, we do not recount (or even remember) the entire content of our experience to date. We are selective about what is included in our story and what is left out, and this is not simply about judging which facts a stranger may or may not know about us. We craft our tale according to a theme; has our life been an adventure story, a comedy or a tragedy? Who are the heroes and anti-heroes? Will it have a happy ending?

The consistency of our narrative demands that we engage in much 'smoothing', choosing and moulding events to fit the theme of our life story. If the theme of a person's self-narrative is 'Life has always dealt me an unfair hand', then events which might be seen as lucky or otherwise positive might be 'smoothed over' in order to fit them to the theme, or left out altogether. This process should not be thought of as necessarily a conscious activity (though it sometimes is). We may not be in a position to articulate readily to ourselves the narrative that we have constructed about our life. It is useful to think of these narratives as the ways we live out our lives as well as the way we privately or publicly tell of them.

Sarbin sees the emergence of narrative structure in human thought as evidence of and dependent upon the perception of time. The fundamental defining feature of a narrative is that it joins events together in a beginning–middle–end sequence which places those events in time as well as space. The concepts of time and space are therefore fundamental to human life, since narratives cannot be built without them. Although narrative structure is seen as basic to human life, it is not clear whether this is 'hard-wired' into the human psyche – that is, whether it is a fundamental 'pre-programmed' part of human nature – or acquired by the kinds of process described by Harré earlier. Sutton-Smith (1986) and Mancuso (1986) show that as children grow up they gradually begin to adopt traditional plot structures in their own story telling and to represent themselves and their actions by using narrative structures.

Gergen and Gergen (1986) have further developed the idea of narrative structure to include the following criteria: a stated goal or valued end-point of the story, narrative events which are represented as having causal connections between them and which relate to the end-point or goal, and movement through time. They go as far as suggesting that we use a limited number of basic narrative forms, such as the 'romance', the 'tragedy' or the 'comedy', each having a characteristic plot shape regarding the rise and fall of fortunes as the story develops.

However, Gergen and Gergen do not only concern themselves with individual psychological functioning. They assert that narrative structure applies just as much to the accounts of science and social science as it does to personal accounts, and they suggest that we address ourselves to the task of understanding how theorists use narrative criteria to enable them to formulate powerful or compelling accounts of human functioning. Although they do not explicitly draw upon work in the poststructuralist tradition, this aspect of their writing bears a resemblance to those who question the 'facticity' of scientific 'knowledge' and seek to lay bare its political implications. Gergen and Gergen's aim is to develop what they term 'Historical Social Psychology', and their major tenet is that psychology and social psychology have traditionally set out with the assumption that the laws of human behaviour and experience can be discovered 'for all time'. Such an assumption, they say, dooms the project to failure, since human life is characterised essentially by change, and we cannot hope to understand ourselves or our predicament if we do not recognise the historical and social contexts of our experience, and indeed the historical, social and therefore political contexts of our theories about human life. In common with other social constructionist writers, they ask not whether our theories of human nature are true or false, but whether they have 'generative potential'. Do they enable us to throw into question the traditional, accepted rules and moral values of our culture and offer fresh alternatives for action? What new narratives in psychology might be useful for people in changing their lives?

In our personal lives, too, our self-narratives have implications well beyond our own functioning. Both Sarbin and the Gergens recognise that the narratives that we construct about ourselves are not simply a private matter. We are heavily dependent upon the willingness of co-actors in the construction of our story. To the extent that we construct our identity, our view of who we are, through narrative accounts, then our stories must be compatible with those of other people who feature in our accounts. For example, a man may have constructed his life history as a tragedy in which his father has the role of thwarting his ambitions, resulting in the son's failure to establish a career. But if the father's life story is a 'progressive' one in which he is portrayed as struggling against all odds and eventually succeeding in raising a healthy family and turning his children into responsible adults, then we can see that the father and son will have great difficulty in playing a part in and supporting each other's self-narratives. We are dependent for our identity upon the willingness of others to support us in our version of events. Narratives are subject to social sanctioning and negotiation.

Similarly, in furnishing accounts of and justifying our actions we are subject to the same limitations. In our attempts to represent ourselves in particular ways, we are dependent upon the willingness of others to allow us to paint a picture of their part in the action that suits our story. Our 'version' of their behaviour must be compatible with their own self-narratives. This feature of narrative construction therefore has fundamental implications for identity; how can we 'bring off' a publicly sanctioned version of ourselves, and what are the limitations imposed on our capacity to do this?

SUMMARY

The views outlined in this chapter suggest that our sense of self is structured around the particular linguistic conventions of our culture. For Harré, this means that selfhood in western industrialised societies is a product both of our use of words such as 'I' and 'me' and of the themes such as choice, decision-making, exhortation and so on that lie at the heart of our linguistic forms. Our sense of self, including our subjective feeling of agency, is something which has crystallised around these linguistic forms, and can be referred to as a (sometimes useful) way of organising our experience, but which is an 'explanatory fiction' rather than a real entity which has effects in the world. Sarbin and the Gergens also focus upon the way that experience is psychologically organised, arguing that human beings are fundamentally story-tellers who experience themselves and their lives in narrative terms.

The person described here has a psychological content, a content which is given by language and framed in narrative. But for Harré the status of this content is definitely that of an *effect* of language. Harré is akin to Potter and Wetherell in his focus not upon finding answers to questions such as whether we have agency or how we make choices, but upon how agency/choice-type talk generates the subjective experience of 'having' agency or choice. However, there is still absent from this account the processes by which linguistic effects become psychologically real. So far, social constructionism has not addressed itself to the question of the psychology that one must theorise in order to show precisely how subjectivity is produced. Human beings, in the view of Sarbin and the Gergens, appear to be active constructive agents, making up stories about themselves and their world, and one must assume that this 'narratory principle' is simply part of human nature.

The struggle to achieve viable identities for ourselves has already been introduced in a previous chapter, and I will return to this issue again in the next chapter. In particular, I will look at the concept of 'positioning' and how different writers in the social constructionist tradition use it to cast light on the social negotiation of identity and the possibilities for personal and social change. As we shall see, the concept of positioning is used by writers of different constructionist persuasions, and the different uses of this term will provide a useful way of contrasting the versions of human subjectivity that are available within the different approaches.

SUGGESTED FURTHER READING

Gergen, K.J. and Gergen, M.M. (1984) 'The social construction of narrative accounts', in K.J. Gergen and M.M. Gergen (eds) *Historical Social Psychology*, Hillsdale, NJ: Lawrence Erlbaum Associates. This chapter, in which Gergen and Gergen put forward their view of the narrative construction of accounts, is part of a useful collection edited by them.

Harré, R. (1983) *Personal Being: A Theory for Individual Psychology*, Oxford: Blackwell.

Harré, R. (1985) 'The language game of self-ascription: a note', in K.J. Gergen and K.E. Davis (eds) *The Social Construction of the Person*, New York: Springer-Verlag.

Harré, R. (1989) 'Language games and the texts of identity', in J. Shotter and K.J. Gergen (eds) *Texts of Identity*, London: Sage.

The last three sources all contain elements of Harré's ideas about the self in language. As he is primarily a philosopher of science, his writing may not be very accessible to some students. In this case, the shorter essays are probably a better starting point than the book.

Harré, R. and Gillett, G. (1994) *The Discursive Mind*, London: Sage. Although primarily a social constructionist account of cognitive psychology, the first three chapters of the book constitute a very readable general introduction.

Sarbin, T.R. (1986) 'The narrative as root metaphor for psychology', in T.R. Sabin (ed.) *Narrative Psychology: The Storied Nature of Human Conduct*, New York: Praeger. This is another chapter which is part of a collection, edited by Sarbin and including a chapter by Gergen and Gergen.

Chapter 9

What does it mean to be a person?

III Subject positions in discourse

At the end of the last chapter, I suggested that people's accounts of themselves, the stories they weave to account for their lives, the things they have done and intend to do and so on, are heavily dependent upon the co-operation of others. Our self-narrative, and indeed any account we may offer of ourselves or our actions, therefore must inevitably be a negotiated one, a joint product which emerges from social interaction. Davies and Harré (1990) suggest 'positioning' as a term to refer to this process of negoti- ated account-production. But the concept of positioning is also used by social constructionist writers (particularly those influ- enced by poststructuralism) to refer to the process by which our identities and ourselves as persons come to be produced by socially and culturally available discourses. Although the idea of positioning bears some surface similarity to the concept of 'role', there are important differences between them. These are described in more detail by Davies and Harré (1990), but focus upon the dynamic nature of positioning and the need to get away from thinking of people as occupying pre-ordained societal 'slots' that come with a pre-written script or set of expected behaviours, which people somehow 'slip on', like an overcoat, over their real selves. In this chapter, I will outline what is meant by positioning both when used to talk about the role of discourses in the production of personhood and identity, and when used in a more interpersonal context.

These two ways of talking about positioning probably imply not so much a difference of opinion as a difference of emphasis. Davies and Harré seem to suggest that these two aspects are operating at the same time; it is just a matter of whether one is currently focussing upon the broad societal aspects of discourse or its manifestation in interactions between specific individuals. They quite clearly hold the human subject to be simultaneously produced by discourse and manipulators of it, and see this as a strength of poststructuralist thinking. As described in an earlier chapter, poststructuralist theory sees the person and her or his identity as a product of the prevailing discourses of selfhood, sexuality, age, race and so on that are culturally available. Discourses, and the discursive practices entailed in them, therefore form the raw materials and manufacturing processes from which people are produced. However, Davies and Harré also see the person as having some room for manoeuvre and choice within those discourses and discursive practices.

Discourses provide us with conceptual repertoires with which we can represent ourselves and others. They provide us with ways of describing a person, such as 'feminine', 'young' and 'disabled'. And each discourse provides a limited number of 'slots' for people. Our discourses of sexuality, for example, give us a very few options, 'gay' and 'straight' being the most readily available. These are the 'subject positions' that are available for people to occupy when they draw on this discourse. Every discourse has implicit within it a number of such 'subject positions', and these obviously have implications for the person who is located within them. As we saw in an earlier chapter, one's actions in the world as well as one's claim to 'voice' depend upon how one is positioned within prevailing discourses. The positions available within discourses bring with them what Davies and Harré refer to as a 'structure of rights'; they provide the possibilities for and the limitations on what we may or may not do and claim for ourselves within a particular discourse; and it is this feature which I will spend some time in outlining next, before returning to an examination of the operation of positioning in the interpersonal context.

THE PERSON AS OCCUPIER OF SUBJECT POSITIONS WITHIN DISCOURSES

Let us briefly recap on some of the points made in the earlier chapter on discourse. We are surrounded by and immersed in discourses. They inhabit all written and spoken material and are embedded in all systems of signification. Even buildings, clothes and consumer goods, to the extent that human beings imbue them

with social meanings, can be 'read' as texts, and can be analysed
to discover the discourses operating within those texts. Since
discourses are identified by the particular way in which they
represent or construct the person (and, of course, all other objects),
we can say that people are constantly subject to numerous
discourses operating in their society. The person can only be a
meaningful entity, both to himself or herself and to others, by
being 'read' in terms of the discourses available in that society.

Positions, power and speaking rights

The concept of positioning offers a way of understanding the
process by which this construction of the person is achieved. The
philosopher Althusser had a very similar idea when he talked
about how we come to take on board ideologies. His central thesis
was that ideology 'interpellates' or 'hails' individuals as subjects.
It shouts to us 'Hey, you there!', and makes us listen as a certain
type of person. When we recognise ourselves as the person hailed
in the ideology, we have already become that person. The idea of
positioning within discourse is rather similar. Discourses address
us as particular kinds of person (as an old person, as a carer, as a
worker, as a criminal and so on), and furthermore we cannot
avoid these subject positions, the representations of ourselves and
others that discourses invite. Our choice is only to accept them or
try to resist them, and if we accept or are unable to resist a particular subject position we are then locked into the system of rights
(including speaking rights) and obligations that are carried with
that position. Parker (1992) gives an illustrative example. A badge
displaying the words 'Dialogue on Diarrhoea' highlights a health
problem for many third world countries, and is sold as part of
a campaign to increase awareness and raise funds. Directed at
western industrialised societies, it may be addressing us through
one of a number of different discourses, each entailing different
subject positions for us and different rights and obligations. A
medical discourse typically contains the positions of those who
offer treatment through their medical knowledge (doctors and
nurses) and of (less knowledgeable) patients who receive their
care. Through this discourse we are addressed as potential carers,
but only to support the work of the 'medically qualified', for
example by volunteering our practical aid or undertaking
medical training. In a medical discourse those without medical

training will be addressed as patients or as non-medics, positions which carry lesser rights to take decisions, make diagnoses, use medical terminology and so on. Or perhaps we feel the 'pull' of the message is in an appeal for charity. A charity discourse draws us in as 'benefactor', and our position entails that we are expected to be understanding and generous. Within this discourse our obligation is to give financial aid and to do so in a non-judgemental spirit. All benefactors have equal status, but have little power when it comes to the distribution and use of donated funds.

Psychology, in so far as it has adopted a scientific discourse, accords researchers and academics a greater claim to truth than the subjects of their study, i.e. lay people (the terms 'scientist' and 'lay person' representing readily available subject positions within a scientific discourse).

The idea of positioning within discourse has been used in the area of gender, showing how women and men are positioned within various discourses and what this has to say about the power relations between them. Hollway (1984) sees heterosexual relations as the primary site where gender difference is reproduced, and therefore sets out to identify a number of heterosexual discourses which contain different positions for women and men. Drawing on her own interview material, she identifies what she feels are three more or less distinct discourses: the 'male-sexual-drive' discourse, the 'permissive' discourse and the 'have/hold' discourse. The 'male-sexual-drive' discourse and the 'have/hold' discourse are of particular interest to us here.

I have already briefly mentioned the 'male-sexual-drive' discourse in an earlier chapter. It centres on the idea that men's sexuality is directly produced by a biological drive, a drive which exists in order to propagate the species. The position implicitly offered for women in this representation of sexuality is as its object; a woman is the object that precipitates men's natural sexual urges, and may be seen as 'trapping' a man by the power of her sexual attraction. The 'male-sexual-drive' discourse is regularly encountered in our culture, and is often used to legitimate such behaviour by men as rape and infidelity. The positions offered to men and women within this discourse can be seen to be very different, involving very different rights and obligations and possibilities for action. Try this 'thought experiment': in your imagination, take up the male or female position offered by the discourse (perhaps try each in turn). How possible does it feel to you that you could appropriately:

complain of sexual frustration?
drink alone in a bar?
look at 'girlie' magazines?
say 'no' to a kiss or other sexual overture?
worry that your clothes look provocative?

My guess is that at least some of these will feel quite different depending upon the subject position you adopt with respect to this discourse.

By contrast, the 'have/hold' discourse legitimates quite a different set of behaviours. It centres on the Christian ideals of monogamy, partnership and family life, and retains the link (seen in the 'male-sexual-drive' discourse) between sexuality and reproduction. It positions women as primarily seeking a long-term emotional commitment through relationships with a husband and children, the women's sexuality being primarily bound up with their desire for motherhood and family life. Representations of men within this discourse focus on their preparedness (or lack of it) to commit themselves to a long-term relationship and to become subject to the obligations it brings. Within this discourse, then, the gender roles are in a sense reversed. Women are the pursuers and men the 'catch'. Hollway (1984) suggests that the effect of the conflict, for men, between the 'male-sexual-drive' discourse and the 'have/hold' discourse is to manufacture a divide between the 'good' girls (whom they marry) and the 'bad' girls (whom they visit in whore-houses), thus maintaining their position in both discourses.

Subject positions and agency

For some writers, such as Althusser and Foucault, the constitutive role of discourse takes centre stage. Althusser believed that all of us live out the requirements of the prevailing ideologies while being under the illusion that we have freely chosen our way of life. In fact, according to Althusser, ideology *is* the experience of being the authors of our own actions. We are simply the bearers of social structures, but experience ourselves as agents. For Foucault too, the human subject appears to be described in terms of the ways in which discourses manifest themselves in texts and practices; discourses live themselves out through people. This way of conceptualising human beings, which amounts to little more than seeing them as puppets operated by structures they cannot see, has been called 'the death of the subject', and refers particularly to the fact that such conceptualisations make it virtually impossible to admit any notion of human agency, i.e. that people are the authors of their own thoughts and actions. This is nicely explained by Craib:

> It is assumed instead that people are the puppets of their ideas, and their actions are determined not by choice and decision but are the outcome of the underlying structure of ideas, the logic of these ideas. If, for example, I am a Christian, I do not speak about Christianity, rather Christianity speaks through me; some structuralists reach the extreme of saying that people do not speak but rather they are spoken (by the underlying structure of the language), that they do not read books but are 'read' by books. They do not create societies but are created by societies.
>
> (Craib, 1984: 109)

This is an extreme position, and not one generally espoused by social constructionists, who for the most part retain some concept of the active, agentic person.

Positions and subjectivity

There is a further feature of Davies and Harré's account of positioning which should be pointed out here, in the context of the overall purpose of this chapter. Positions in discourse are also seen as providing us with the content of our subjectivity. Once we take up a position within a discourse (and some of these positions entail a long-term occupation by the person, like gender or fatherhood), we then inevitably come to experience the world and ourselves from the vantage point of that perspective. Once we take up a subject position in discourse, we have available to us a particular, limited set of concepts, images, metaphors, ways of speaking, self-narratives and so on that we take on as our own. This entails both an emotional commitment on our part to the categories of person to which we are allocated and see ourselves as belonging (such as male, grandfather or worker) and the development of an appropriate system of morals (rules of right and wrong). Our sense of who we are and what it is therefore possible and not possible for us to do, what it is right and appropriate for us to do, and what it is wrong and inappropriate for us to do thus all derive from our occupation of subject positions within discourse.

Some subject positions are more temporary or even fleeting, and thus 'who we are' is constantly in flux, always dependent upon the changing flow of positions we negotiate within social interaction. Thus, in this account, our subjective experience of ourselves, of being the person we take ourselves to be, is given by the totality of subject positions, some permanent, some temporary and some fleeting, that we take up in discourse.

POSITIONING IN THE INTERPERSONAL CONTEXT

Defining the situation

Just as negotiating narratives involves the co-operation of others, so this remains true if we now characterise the negotiation process in terms of 'positioning'. Thus, we may ourselves adopt a position by drawing upon a particular discourse, or we may 'assign' positions to other speakers through the part that we give them in our story. For example, a person may treat someone's remark as 'offering sympathy', and respond to it by adopting the position of 'victim'. However, the original remark may not have been intended in this way, and the speaker may not wish to be positioned as 'one who would offer sympathy in such cases'. The result may be that an attempt is made to re-define the speaker's first remark and therefore offer new positions for both speakers.

Thus subject positions of many kinds are drawn into the play from moment to moment, and these may be offered, accepted, claimed or resisted by the participants. It follows that in any interchange between people, there is a constant monitoring of the 'definition of the situation' that each participant is struggling to bring off. Participants' understanding of 'what this conversation is about' will radically affect their perception of what subject positions are available to them and whether they wish to claim or resist those positions. An example I gave in an earlier chapter described the 'struggle after meaning' that occurred between a couple on a car journey. We could now say that these two people were engaged in claiming or rejecting the positions implicitly offered in each other's 'definition of the situation'.

Davies and Harré show how different constructions of an inter-action can offer radically different subject positions, which in turn entail radically different sets of rights and obligations for the participants. And, like Potter and Wetherell, the authors do not see such positioning as necessarily intentional (though it some-times is). People may therefore become enmeshed in the subject positions implicit in their talk without necessarily having intended to position each other in particular ways. But Davies and Harré make the important point that we would do well to recognise and develop an awareness of the potential implications of the narratives/discourses we adopt in our dealings with others. As well as being less likely to position others in ways we did not intend, we may also gain for ourselves a useful strategy in our own struggles with personal identity and change. I will return to this issue later in the chapter.

Positions and power

This concern with the details of positioning in the interpersonal context is not about how we can bring off smooth interactions (though it has implications here), but is about how positions offered, accepted or resisted in everyday talk are the discursive practices by which discourses and their associated power impli-cations are brought to life. When we position ourselves or others during conversation, we are doing something that has effects which go beyond that immediate social event. Everyday conver-sation, even down to the apparent inconsequentiality of exchanges about the weather or how your children are getting on at school, are therefore far from trivial and represent an important arena where identities are fashioned and power relations played out. In fact, the claim that such talk is trivial can be used as a powerful device. Feminists who believe that language is central to women's oppression have often made this point. For example, a woman who complains that suggestive comments from her male work colleagues constitute sexual harassment may have her complaint 'defused' by the response that the comments were 'only a bit of fun' or 'just a joke' and that therefore the problem lies not in their comments but in her lack of a sense of humour. The success of such a strategy depends upon these comments being represented as trivial and therefore harmless. 'Real' oppression, if it exists, is represented as lying elsewhere (perhaps in the laws regarding employment and pay), a site apparently removed from the day-to-day commonplaces of conversation. If we are going to take seriously the view that language is a crucial site of identity nego-tiation and of power relations, then we can no longer afford to view as trivial the arguments over whether words such as 'black-leg' or 'mankind' should be outlawed.

The concept of 'positioning', then, affords a way of looking at both how people are subject to discourse and how this subjectivity is negotiated in interpersonal life. Walkerdine (1981) gives a good example which illustrates this dual nature of positioning. Using her own recordings of child–teacher interactions in a nursery school, she shows how children and teachers are engaged in a struggle to position themselves and each other in different discourses, and the power effects that are brought about by this positioning. She quotes an exchange between the nursery teacher, Miss Baxter, and two 4-year-old boys, Sean and Terry. I have repro-duced the entire episode here:

> The sequence begins when Annie takes a piece of Lego to add on to a construction that she is building. Terry tries to take it away from her to use himself and she resists. He says:
>
> Terry: You're a stupid cunt, Annie.
>
> The teacher tells him to stop and Sean tries to mess up another child's construction. The teacher tells him to stop. Then Sean says:
>
> Sean: Get out of it Miss Baxter paxter.
> Terry: Get out of it knickers Miss Baxter.
> Sean: Get out of it Miss Baxter paxter.
> Terry: Get out of it Miss Baxter the knickers paxter knickers, bum.
> Sean: Knickers, shit, bum.
> Miss B: Sean, that's enough, you're being silly.
> Sean: Miss Baxter, knickers, show your knickers.
> Terry: Miss Baxter, show your bum off.
> (they giggle)
> Miss B: I think you're being very silly.
> Terry: Shit Miss Baxter, shit Miss Baxter.
> Sean: Miss Baxter, show your knickers your bum off.

Sean: Take all your clothes off, your bra off.

Terry: Yeah, and take your bum off, take your wee-wee off, take your clothes, your mouth off.

Sean: Take your teeth out, take your head off, take your hair off, take your bum off. Miss Baxter the paxter knickers taxter.

Miss B: Sean, go and find something else to do, please.

(Walkerdine, 1981)

Walkerdine uses this example to show how as individuals we are constantly subject to an interplay of different discourses, each with its own structure of rights, obligations and possibilities for action, and each carrying identity and power implications. She is primarily arguing against a traditional Marxist analysis of education, which would see the teacher as uncomplicatedly in a position of power over the children, who have fewer rights and freedoms. In such an analysis, the children are straightforwardly oppressed by education, and by its representative here, the teacher. But in this example, the children are seen to seize power temporarily and to render their teacher relatively powerless by their ability to draw upon the discourse of sexuality and to position themselves and their teacher within it. The two boys, by their sexual comments, temporarily locate themselves as male and their teacher as female within a discourse of sexuality which affords them some supremacy. Miss Baxter ceases to signify primarily as a teacher (the relatively powerful position in the teacher–child educational pairing) and for a time becomes positioned as 'woman' in a discourse of sexuality, thus rendering her as 'sex object' to the young boys.

The teacher's response to their talk appears weak and ineffective ('I think you're being very silly') and does not help her to resist the subject position she is being offered. Walkerdine explains the teacher's response in terms of the prevailing discourse of nursery education within which she experiences herself as a teacher. Nursery education is seen as a process of allowing the child's natural potential to unfold through the teacher's nurturance and guidance. Free expression, denying the distinction between work and play, is seen as the process by which the child can develop naturally. Within this framework, the teacher is there to monitor the child's unfolding development, and to steer it gently in appropriate directions. A strict, regimented or controlling teacher is out of place here, and Miss Baxter's later comments about the children's talk explain her response: 'The kind of expressions are quite normal for this age ... As long as they're not being too silly or bothering anybody, its just natural and should be left ... coming out with that kind of expression is very natural' (Walkerdine, 1981: 169). The boys' talk, within this discourse of nursery education, were therefore represented as part of a natural developmental phase, and therefore simply to be monitored rather than resisted by the teacher. One could therefore say that prevailing discourses of sexuality and of nursery education came together in this episode and provided an opportunity for the young boys to reverse the usual power relations operating in school settings. This example nicely shows not just how the positions offered, accepted or resisted are of importance in understanding how people manage social interactions, but how positions are drawn from discourses which are constantly operating as it were 'behind the scenes' of all social interactions. Opportunities for identity negotiation and for grasping power occur as we position ourselves and others within a variety of discourses in the shifting flow of social interaction.

The discursive positions on offer to us during social interaction may therefore play a central role in the extent to which we are able to negotiate satisfactory identities for ourselves, and in our ability (physically and morally) to behave and and to take action as we would like. To the extent that material conditions and social practices are inextricably bound up in discourse, then our ability to, say, earn a living, go out at night, tell people what to do or refuse to do what others say depends upon the positions in discourses that we can take up or resist. It follows therefore that an understanding of positioning and an ability to use it skilfully could be important tools in people's efforts to change themselves or their circumstances.

POSITIONING AND CHANGE

As Burr and Butt (1993) have argued, the first step towards personal change, within this framework of discursive positioning, is to recognise the discourses (and the positions provided by them) that are currently shaping our subjectivity. Such a recognition can be beneficial in itself, by re-locating problems away from an intra-psychic domain and into a societal one. For example, 'depression' is a term which locates problems within the internal psychology of the individual. A woman may complain of depression, feeling that she cannot cope with her life. Perhaps she feels that she is a bad mother because she frequently loses her temper with her young children, or that she is an inadequate daughter because she is reluctant to care for her own elderly mother. But in re-casting the problem at a societal level rather than at the level of the individual, a different analysis emerges. Such an analysis may suggest that the woman see herself as oppressed rather than depressed. The discourses of motherhood, femininity, family life and so on actively encourage women to engage in practices which are not necessarily in their own psychological, social and economic best interests. Thinking of oneself as oppressed rather than depressed fosters a different view of oneself and of how to attack one's problems. It may not solve those problems; the woman in the example will still have to decide what to do about her elderly mother, but she may not feel so conflict-ridden and guilty.

An examination of the discourses and positions available to us may help us to work towards occupying positions in discourses which are less personally damaging. The woman who fears she is a bad mother may be helped by recognising the 'good mother' as a discourse with political implications. The popular representation of the 'good mother' as one who spends time with her children when they are young and who sacrifices her own needs to theirs helps to keep women out of full-time employment and ensures their economic dependency upon men. But different and competing discourses of motherhood, and of 'good motherhood', exist. The task is therefore one of finding ways of resisting being positioned in personally damaging motherhood discourses, and how to claim positions in discourses which are beneficial. In short, it means finding ways that you can 'do' good motherhood in a way that is acceptable to you. For example, we might represent the essential task of motherhood as 'helping one's children to become self-reliant'. While preserving the idea that mothers should nurture and guide their offspring, such a representation allows a mother to go out to work and still claim the position of 'good' rather than 'bad' mother.

However, this is not to say that such changes can be accomplished easily. To the extent that prevailing or dominant discourses are often tied to social arrangements and practices which support the status quo and maintain the positions of powerful groups, then in challenging such discourses and resisting the positions they offer we are also implicitly challenging their associated social practices, structures and power relations. We can therefore expect to find some degree of resistance to our attempts at change. For example, a woman may want to become more 'assertive', but behaving in an assertive manner is not consistent with dominant discourses of femininity and womanhood. One could say that the absence of assertiveness and other instrumental 'qualities' from the femininity package-deal means that such psychological repertoires are not easily available as a resource to women, and makes it easier for men to hold the reins of society. So in 'becoming more assertive' a woman is implicitly taking on more than a struggle to change the nature of her social interactions within her immediate social circle. However, recognition of this can at least help us to anticipate, understand and counter such resistance when it occurs.

On an interpersonal level, we can work towards change firstly by becoming more aware of the positions we are being offered and that we offer to others in our interactions with them. We can then devise strategies for how unacceptable positions might be resisted and positions in alternative discourses taken up. This would involve deciding how to change one's response to particular conversational gambits, or when to remain silent (silence may well be a particularly useful way of resisting positions we do not want to accept).

SUBJECTIVITY AND POSITIONING

Let us now summarise what the human subject looks like within this framework of discursive positioning. The person can be described by the sum total of the subject positions in discourse they currently occupy. The fact that some of these positions are fleeting or in a state of flux means that our identity is never fixed but always in process, always open to change. The subject positions that we occupy bring with them a structure of rights and obligations, they legislate for what 'that kind of person' may or may not reasonably do or say. But according to Davies and Harré this amounts to more than an external set of rules about appropriate behaviour. Not only do our subject positions constrain and shape what we do, they are taken on as part of our psychology, so that they provide us also with our sense of self, the ideas and metaphors with which we think, and the self-narratives we use to talk and think about ourselves. We thus have an emotional commitment to and investment in our subject positions which goes beyond mere rule-following.

The extent of our personal choice and agency in taking up subject positions is a matter for debate. Davies and Harré, and writers concerned to apply discourse theory to issues of personal and social change, are generally committed to the view that the person has some negotiating power and room for manoeuvre. They stress the choices that are available to the person in how he or she may take up or resist the positions on offer to him or her, and to this extent the person can be seen as a negotiator of his or her own identity.

The extreme structuralist view, by comparison, sees human subjects as secondary to and as products of the discourses that structure their lives. The 'content' of such a being is hard to imagine; indeed whatever psychological processes are attributed to it can only have the status of by-products. They can never have much explanatory value when it comes to understanding what people are like or why they behave in the ways they do. According to this view, once we have laid bare the structures and discourses which are currently producing human social life, there will be nothing left to explain.

This extreme view is problematic for a number of reasons (see Craib, 1984, for a good account of the arguments concerning agency), but it is also paradoxical when it comes to the application of its own research programme. In order to understand society and social life, we must identify and lay bare the discourses that are currently 'pulling our strings'. However, if this is the case, how is such a task possible? How can we stand outside of and regard the structures that are producing us? The very project of discourse analysis becomes problematic. The alternative view, that we both actively produce and manipulate, *and* are products of, discourse allows us the possibility of personal and social change through our capacity to identify, understand and resist the discourses that we are also subject to.

However, the processes by which change, particularly societal change, may be brought about have not been clearly articulated, and this is an area which still needs a good deal of thought. We do not yet appear to be in a position to make any detailed recommendations, based on an understanding of discourse and positioning, for how individuals or groups might facilitate change.

THE PROBLEM OF DESIRE

One of the biggest problems that some of these accounts run into is how one explains the desires, wants, hopes and fantasies of a person and their role in the choices that people make in their lives. To say that people are negotiators of positions, or that their subjectivity is formed by discourses, says nothing about how these processes are supposed to operate. In addition, it fails to explain properly such phenomena, which are after all very real experiences for us, and relegates them to a kind of 'side-effect' of discourse. But most importantly, it fails to explain why, even in the face of an understanding of the implications of discourse for our identity and the power relations in which we are thereby embedded, we do not feel free to choose an alternative way of life. For example, a woman may believe that discourses of motherhood constrain and control women, or that sexual relations with men are at the heart of women's oppression. Yet she may still desperately wish for a child, or be unable to quell her desire for a sexual relationship with a man. Chodorow (1978), writing from a psychoanalytic position, made this point a long time ago. She argued that most existing explanations of why women mother (perhaps they are 'rewarded' for gender-appropriate behaviour, or they have to do it because, in general, men refuse to) ignore the fact that you cannot make someone into a good mother unless she wants to do it and has a sense of her own self that is consistent with the demands of mothering.

In order to address these problems, some social constructionist writers, such as Hollway (1989) and Walkerdine (1987), have built psychoanalytic concepts into their accounts of subjectivity (in fact in the case of Hollway, it may be more accurate to describe her approach as a psychoanalytic account with discourse built into it). It is probably true to say that it is social constructionists operating primarily from within the area of gender who have drawn most heavily upon psychoanalysis, and as we shall see this is because psychoanalysis offers a view of the person as non-unitary and non-rational, and at the same time takes sexuality as its starting point.

Whether psychoanalytic ideas can be legitimately combined with social constructionism is a matter of some debate. It is quite easy for psychoanalysis to promote a slide back into essentialism, as it traditionally deals in terms of pre-existing motives, purposes and needs residing inside the individual, and therefore may be legitimately seen as 'absolutely counter to social constructionist principles' (Kitzinger, personal communication). However, the use of psychoanalysis does represent an attempt to come to grips with some important issues which are left largely unresolved by social constructionism, and it is therefore appropriate to say something here about the kinds of idea that readers will meet in the social constructionist literature.

The experience of conflicting desires, of knowing that something is bad for you but wanting it anyway, is of course entirely compatible with psychoanalytic thinking. Psychoanalysis is one of the few psychologies which does not assume at its centre the single, unified and coherent human subject. Psychoanalysis is fundamentally based upon the idea that humans are split, conflicted and therefore non-unitary beings. The conscious mind is dissociated from the unconscious, which nevertheless asserts itself through our behaviour and our dreams. This 'undercover operation' of the unconscious made psychoanalysis attractive to some Marxist theorists, who saw it as explaining how people could live in a state of false consciousness.

One form of psychoanalysis which has been taken up with enthusiasm by many feminist and social constructionist writers is that of the French analyst Lacan. Lacan has devoted himself to a re-reading of Freud that is very much in the French intellectual tradition which also fostered Saussure's structuralism and the writing of poststructuralists such as Foucault and Derrida. Lacan's emphasis, as a psychoanalyst, upon the role of language and culture in psychosexual development is certainly idiosyncratic, but one that is sympathetic to many of the concerns of social constructionism.

Lacan's writing is notoriously difficult and impenetrable, and it seems likely that at least some of those appropriating his ideas are relying upon secondary sources (themselves often difficult enough). I shall do no more here than attempt to give a brief outline of the features of Lacan's psychoanalysis which have been taken up by social constructionists, in particular his insistence upon the non-unitary subject, the importance of language and the emergence of sexuality and desire.

Until it reaches the age of approximately six to eighteen months, the infant can be described as a heterogeneous, shifting and centreless mass of needs and sensations. At this stage, there is no sense of being separate from the world or from the mother, and there is certainly no sense of being a separate person in one's own right. All sensation and experience appears as a complete whole for the infant. But around the time of its first birthday, this all changes. The infant will up to this time have been cared for by a mother or other adults and siblings who have responded to the child *as if* it were a unified, coherent being. At some point soon, perhaps by catching sight of its reflection in a mirror, the child 'mistakes' this visual bodily appearance of unity and misinterprets it as representing a coherent, unified being. Lacan refers to this as the 'mirror stage' of development. The child has internalised the 'messages' about coherence and unity reflected by people and coming also from its own physical appearance, and from now on will mistakenly think of itself in this way.

However, at this stage the child is still bound up in a kind of symbiotic relationship with its mother, in which it has not yet developed the sense of being separate from her. According to Lacan, this sense of separateness, which is at the very base of our notion of the individual, can come about only when the child acquires language. The sense of being a person in one's own right is made possible by language, because language is founded on a system of oppositions (as also argued by Derrida) such as 'I/you' and 'self/other'. In acquiring language, the child must think of itself as an 'I' or a 'self' as opposed to 'you' or 'other', and therefore at this point becomes forever separated from other people and the exterior world in the way it must experience itself. In fact a self can only ever exist in relation to what is *not self*, i.e. 'other'. In Lacan's terms, the child is now beginning to take up its place in the 'Symbolic Order', the order of culture and language.

But the symbolic, the culture that pre-exists the child's entry into the world, is not only a realm of language. It is also a realm of rules, of moral laws, prohibitions and customs which will soon be imposed upon the child, making it fully a social being. For Lacan, this happens decisively in the shape of the Oedipus complex. This complex can be seen as part of the wider phenomenon of the 'incest taboo', a widespread cultural prohibition upon sexual relations between near relatives (and not only between sons and mothers, as in the case of Oedipus). This taboo is seen as delivered upon the child by its father, who appears as the representative of the laws, prohibitions and powers of culture. The child is forced to recognise sexual difference (based upon the absence or presence of the phallus) and to take up a position as masculine or feminine in relation to others, and the cultural prohibition on incest thus makes the child fearful of its own desire for its mother. This desire is repressed, it is split off from the child's conscious sense of self, and thus founds the unconscious. The person is therefore a fragmented, split and conflictual being.

In coming face to face with these laws and prohibitions, expressed through the cultural categories of male and female, of masculine and feminine and of sexuality, the child is forced to recognise itself as a gendered, sexual being. Thus, the child's full entry into the symbolic realm, the realm where it is finally fully constituted as a separate, unified human being embedded in social relationships with other human beings, is achieved through the child's very constitution and recognition of itself as gendered and sexual. The sense of self is therefore inextricably tied in with gender and sexuality.

However, the unconscious remains as a constant reminder of what has been lost; at some level we are all aware that, in order to become separate, coherent selves, we have made an artificial division between the interior and exterior world, between self and other, and between male and female. At some level we feel a desire to return to that amorphous infant state before the mirror stage, before we became a split-off bit of consciousness, and we are therefore forever locked into a constant cycle of desire for the 'other' that we relinquished in order to be a self. Desire can therefore never be satisfied once and for all, since the wholeness that we seek is an impossibility.

Lacan's account thus asserts that the human subject is constructed through its entry into a symbolic, linguistic realm (and this is of course consistent with social constructionism). But it also explains the development of a gendered sexuality. The processes which produce this sexuality (the Oedipus complex) also simultaneously produce desire. Our sexuality is therefore forever linked to pursuing the satisfaction of a desire which can never be fulfilled.

However, Lacanian psychoanalysis has been criticised, primarily on the basis of its 'phallocentrism'. Lacan simply assumes that sexuality is organised around perceived sexual difference, and that this difference is constituted by the presence or absence of a penis. Women are therefore defined in terms of having a lack or absence.

This assumption of the importance of the phallus has been criti-cised, and I think justifiably so, particularly by some feminists.The account also seems to be pessimistically deterministic. The human subject appears to be wholly formed by and at the mercy of cultural forces, forces which are explicitly patriarchal. The 'Law of the Father' (i.e. the cultural laws and prohibitions of a society) appears to be inescapable, and Lacan therefore seems to offer no challenge to the status quo. In addition, Lacan's account suffers from the same difficulty as other forms of psychoanalysis, and that is the apparent impossibility of either supporting or refuting it with research evidence.

Nevertheless, Lacan provides a useful account of subjectivity, which attempts to explain how cultural forces come to operate at the deepest levels of a person's experience. Writers such as Hollway (1984) and Walkerdine (1987) have produced some interesting analyses based on a combination of Lacan's ideas and discourse. For example, Walkerdine (1987) shows how the stories in girls' comics key into fundamental psychological issues and conflicts for girls and help to form and produce female desire along traditional, heterosexual lines, in preparation for their developing sexuality in adolescence. Some French feminists in the psychoanalytic tradition have taken up Lacan's ideas and reformulated them in ways which they believe are more consis-tent with a feminist viewpoint.

SUGGESTED FURTHER READING

Davies, B. and Harré, R. (1990) 'Positioning: the discursive production of selves', *Journal for the Theory of Social Behaviour* 20 (1): 43–63. This is one of the few detailed accounts of the concept of positioning, and contains a very good illustrative example.

Frosh, S. (1987) *The Politics of Psychoanalysis: An Introduction to Freudian and Post-Freudian Theory*, London: Macmillan. This contains the clearest brief account of Lacan that I have found.

Hollway, W. (1984) 'Gender difference and the production of subjec-tivity', in J. Henriques, W. Hollway, C. Urwin, C. Venn and V. Walkerdine *Changing the Subject: Psychology, Social Regulation and Subjectivity*, London: Methuen. In this chapter, Hollway uses positions in discourse combined with Lacanian ideas in an analysis of gender.

Walkerdine, V. (1981) 'Sex, power and pedagogy', *Screen Education* 38: 14–23. Reprinted in M. Arnot and G. Weiner (eds) (1987) *Gender and the Politics of Schooling*, London: Hutchinson. Walkerdine examines the positions available for children and women within prevailing discourses of gender and education.

Chapter 10

What do discourse analysts do?

If we take on board the social constructionist arguments concerning the nature of personhood, the role of language in identity, subjectivity and social life, the relationship between the individual and society, and the historical and cultural specificity of traditional psychology and social psychology, it becomes evident that the aims and practices of social enquiry must be transformed radically. We cannot investigate the psychological and social world using our old assumptions and practices, because their focus on internal psychic structures and processes such as attitudes and personality traits is inappropriate. We must also build into our new practices of scientific enquiry our understanding of how the 'knowledge' produced within the traditional scientific paradigm is a function of a power imbalance between researchers and the objects of their study. Above all, our new research practices must take language as their focus of interest, since the uses and effects of language are of central importance to social constructionists.

Concern with these issues has led to new developments in social psychological research and a flurry of research activity in what is often referred to as 'discourse analysis'. There are some points to be raised here, before proceeding to describe what is meant by discourse analysis and how it is carried out.

THEORETICAL CONSIDERATIONS

Firstly, it is necessary to outline some of the theoretical assumptions underlying the approach which are of particular relevance in a research context.

Objectivity

Researchers can claim truthfulness for their findings by recourse to the supposed objectivity of scientific method. Experimenters, within the traditional scientific paradigm, are able to stand back from their own humanity and reveal the objective nature of the phenomena under study without bias and without 'contaminating' the results with 'leakage' from their own personal involvement. However, within a social constructionist framework, the 'objectivity-talk' of scientists becomes just part of the discourse of science through which a particular version (and vision) of human life is constructed.

But objectivity is an impossibility, since each of us, of necessity, must encounter the world from some perspective or other (from where we stand) and the questions we come to ask about that world, our theories and hypotheses, must also of necessity arise from the assumptions that are embedded in our perspective. No human being can step outside of her or his humanity and view the world from no position at all, which is what the idea of objectivity suggests, and this is just as true of scientists as of everyone else. The task of researchers therefore becomes to acknowledge and even to work with their own intrinsic involvement in the research process and the part that this plays in the results that are produced. Researchers must view the research as necessarily a co-production between themselves and the people they are researching. For example, in an interview it can be readily seen how the researcher's own assumptions must inform what questions are asked and how, and that the interviewer as a human being cannot be seen as an inanimate writing pad or machine that records the interviewee's responses uncontaminated by human interaction.

Researcher and researched

As discussed in an earlier chapter, within a social constructionist framework traditional psychology, as a scientific enterprise, is seen as making powerful truth claims. The discourse and rhetoric of science give the findings of psychological research the stamp of 'knowledge' or 'truth', and put the psychologist or researcher in a relatively powerful position with respect to those people whom they are researching; the researcher's 'version' of events has greater 'warrant' and is given more 'voice' than that of the 'subject', whose experience is interpreted and given (sometimes quite different) meanings by the researcher.

If the scientist's or researcher's account of a phenomenon is seen to receive the stamp of 'knowledge' or 'truth' as a result of the 'warranting voice' of science, we must then acknowledge that other accounts, for example those of respondents in interviews, must be equally valid in principle. There no longer appears to be a good reason to privilege the account or 'reading' of the researcher above that of anyone else, and this puts the researcher and the researched in a new relation to each other. Subjects' own account of their experiences can no longer be given an alternative interpretation by researchers who then offer their reading as truth. In the development of alternative research practices, the validity of the participants' accounts must be incorporated. This is part of what is referred to as 'reflexivity'.

Reflexivity

Reflexivity is a term which is widely used in social constructionist writing, and, confusingly, is not necessarily used in the same way by different writers. As well as referring to the way that the theory re-constitutes the role of respondents, their relationship to the researcher and the status of their accounts, the term is also used in at least two other ways. Firstly, reflexivity is used to draw attention to the fact that, when someone gives an account of an event, that account is simultaneously a description of the event *and* part of the event (because of the constitutive nature of talk). Secondly, and this is the more widely used meaning, reflexivity refers to the fact that social constructionism itself is not exempt from the critical stance it brings to bear on other theories. Social constructionism, as a body of theory and practice, therefore must recognise itself as just as much a social construction as are other ways of accounting. Some writers are interested in analysing their own writing, reflexively discussing how their own accounts have been constructed (Ashmore, 1989; Mulkay, 1985). There is more on reflexivity later in this chapter.

The aims of research

Social constructionist theory, particularly that influenced by post-structuralism, often tends (either deliberately or by default) to adopt a relativist position in which one cannot search for truth (i.e. objectivity) but must accept the existence of many alternative constructions of events. If this is the case, the project of social science can no longer be to uncover the truth about people or society. Many social constructionist researchers believe that the aims of research should become not the discovery of 'facts', but the mobilisation of the research process towards a different goal. The goal becomes a pragmatic and political one, a search not for truth but for any usefulness that the researcher's 'reading' of a phenomenon might have in bringing about change for those who need it. Research thus becomes 'action research' (research which has change and intervention as its explicit aim) and a political activity. For example, a study in which the researcher claimed that children in education are caught up in oppressive power relations would be evaluated not in terms of whether this was an accurate or truthful account of reality, but in terms of how useful and liberatory such an analysis might be to children themselves. This suggested change in the goal of social science research has led to criticisms from traditional psychology, which has always regarded itself as apolitical. However, as we saw earlier, there are plenty of good reasons for regarding traditional psychology as being just as politically loaded, but covertly so.

Not all social constructionists take such a political stance, as we shall see, and many are more interested in investigating the workings of language and the construction of accounts for their own sake. Such an approach can be seen as valid, in terms of building up a new model of psychology and of social psychology, and identifying new ways of understanding social phenomena. But those with an explicitly political agenda may well feel uncomfortable with research which appears to deny or at least disregard the power issues embedded in discourse. A considerable danger is that when it comes to social constructionist research which purports to analyse social phenomena, the 'best' analysis may well turn out to be no more than what is currently 'politically correct'. The absence of objective criteria for assessing the worth of social constructionist research is a problem endemic to the area, though one which writers such as Potter and Wetherell (1987) have attempted to resolve.

Social constructionism and discourse analysis

A social constructionist theoretical position does not necessarily mean that one must use a discourse analytic approach in one's research, or that to use a discourse analytic approach means that one must be a social constructionist. Social constructionism as a loose collection of theoretical perspectives, and discourse analysis as an approach to doing social research, do not map onto each other in a one-to-one fashion. Social constructionists may validly use other qualitative or even quantitative methods in their research and, as Burman and Parker (1993) point out, researchers who are not social constructionists may 'discover' that they have been doing discourse analysis without labelling it as such. Having said this, it seems to be the case that discourse analysis has been enthusiastically adopted by many social constructionists as an approach to research.

I have referred to discourse analysis as 'an approach to research' as I wanted to avoid talking of it as a particular method or technique. Discourse analysis is unlike the majority of existing traditional methods of social scientific enquiry, since it is not possible to describe it adequately in 'recipe-type' terms. For example, if researchers want to carry out a controlled laboratory experiment involving the action of some variable upon people in a 'matched samples' design, they can consult research methodology texts which will provide clear instructions about sampling strategies and how to control for unwanted variables, as well as suggestions for appropriate statistical analysis. If researchers want to develop a questionnaire, again clear recommendations are available for how precisely one should go about designing questions, piloting them and so on. Although some guidelines for doing discourse analysis do exist (in particular, see Potter and Wetherell's (1987) very helpful step-by-step guide), these necessarily fall short of concrete 'how-you-do-it' instructions, since the nature of discourse analysis itself is subjective and interpretative.

Lastly, but importantly, the term 'discourse analysis' is an umbrella which covers a wide variety of actual research practices with quite different aims and theoretical backgrounds. All take language as their focus of interest, and therefore use as their basic materials such things as interview transcripts, recordings of 'natural' conversations, extracts from books and so on, though different 'species' of discourse analysis vary in terms of what it is they are looking for in a piece of text, and the specific methods by which they carry out their analysis. The 'discourse analysis' undertaken by those in the tradition of conversation analysis, for example, is not especially informed by or concerned with social constructionist theory, although the analytic method it adopts has influenced others who do take a social constructionist approach. (See Potter *et al.*, 1990, for a brief overview of the different discourse analytic approaches and their origins.)

For the purposes of this chapter, I will concentrate upon the work of researchers who have used a version of discourse analysis to research questions concerning the construction of accounts, the performance of social acts through language, and the identification of the discourses and interpretative repertoires which we draw upon in our interactions and which also may have identity implications. Even within this much narrower working definition of discourse analysis there are some debates and tensions which appear to set one approach against another, and I will address these differences as they arise. In particular, Potter *et al.* (1990) make a distinction between 'the analysis of discourses', which they associate with the work of writers such as Parker and Burman, and their own work, which they refer to as 'discourse analysis'.

For the purposes of organising the remainder of this chapter, I shall talk firstly of the approach generally known as 'deconstruction', within which I subsume 'the analysis of discourses' as referred to by Potter *et al.* (1990), and then go on to look at the different emphasis of those doing 'discourse analysis'. It must be pointed out, however, that such distinctions and attention to difference are by no means widely adopted, so that the reader is likely to be confused by the great variety in approaches adopted by research articles which advertise themselves as using 'discourse analysis'.

DECONSTRUCTION

Deconstruction refers to attempts to take apart texts and see how they are constructed in such a way as to present particular images of people and their actions. Deconstruction can be thought of as taking several different forms.

Revealing contradictions

In the sense of this term as it derives from Derrida, deconstruction would mean looking at texts in a particular area or discipline (e.g. scientific texts), revealing how they contain 'hidden' internal contradictions, and making the absent or repressed meanings present for the reader, showing how we are led by the text into accepting the assumptions it contains. For example, Squire (1990) points out that the traditional 'passive' language of psychological research reports obscures the activity of the researcher. Psychologists write that 'an experiment was performed', rather than that they performed an experiment, or that 'subjects were exposed to stimulus material' rather than that they (the researchers) gave the subjects the material. Squire comments:

But the authority of the absent investigator lies behind every passive textual construction. It is he or she who decides hypotheses and methods, and draws conclusions from results. The investigation tries to increase scientific order and truth at the expense of the chaos and errors in the field.

(Squire, 1990: 40)

The felt absence of the investigator achieved by the passive style adopted in psychological reports helps to construct the image of objectivity that is necessary to traditional concepts of psychology as a science, and is here brought to full presence by Squire through her deconstruction of psychological texts.

Billig (1990) focusses upon the deconstruction of texts and accounts by analysing their rhetorical nature. He argues that texts (including what psychologists and other scientists write and say, as well as the everyday conversations of ordinary people) are constructed using rhetorical devices. He argues that our accounts are suffused with our attempts to persuade each other of the power of our arguments, and that they are therefore argumentative in nature:

In persuasive communication, speakers and writers attempt to present their discourse as reasonable by giving justifications for their position and by countering objections with criticisms. In short, they produce reasoned arguments and rhetoric involves the production of argumentative discourse, which in a literal sense is justified and reasonable.

(Billig, 1990: 51)

So the analysis of rhetoric looks at all the ways in which we use linguistic devices to present a justifiable account. And our accounts are always located within a context of public debate and argument. Accounts are simultaneously arguing for one position and against other positions, although what is being rejected may not be explicitly stated in the account (as in Squire's example above). Thus, for example, when we are asked for our attitude towards something we must necessarily adopt a stance towards the alternative(s). So in deconstructing accounts, according to Billig, we must look not only at what is being said, but also at what is (perhaps only implicitly) being rejected. We can therefore deconstruct or take apart any kind of text, from an ordinary conversation to a scientific report, and expose the way that the particular view of life that it contains is rhetorically constructed.

The archaeology of knowledge

A second form of deconstruction is theoretically allied to the kind of poststructuralist theory that I have outlined earlier in this book, and draws on Foucault's notion of 'genealogy'. This concerns itself with tracing the development of present ways of understanding, of current discourses and representations of people and society, to show how current 'truths' have come to be constituted, how they are maintained and what power relations are carried by them. Rose (1990) performs such a Foucauldian deconstruction on the discipline of social psychology, showing how its concepts and practices can be seen as part of the general phenomenon of the emergence of 'the individual' as understood in western industrialised societies.

The analysis of discourses

This second form of deconstruction is allied to 'the analysis of discourses', whereby prevailing discourses of, say, gender, sexuality, disability and so on are examined and their identity and power implications brought to the fore. This might involve identifying the subject positions offered by different discourses, and the identity and political implications of these. For example, Hollway's (1984) identification of the 'male sexual drive' and 'have/hold' discourses serve to show how men and women are invited into different kinds of self-experience with different behavioural implications. Walkerdine's (1981) analysis of a nursery school interaction is also in this vein, as is Stenner's (1993) analysis in which he looks at the construction of 'jealousy' in accounts given of their relationship by a couple whom he interviewed. Any piece of text, in principle, could be deconstructed to lay bare the discourses operating through it. For example, Macnaghten (1993) analysed the spoken and written text of a public enquiry over a planning application for a landfill site (a tip), and identified a number of 'discourses of nature' which were being mobilised towards the particular ends of the enquiry participants. He identified these as 'nature as wilderness', 'nature as passive visual harmony', 'nature as the visual harmony of activities' and 'nature as ecological balance'. These different discourses imported with them, as one might expect, quite different implications for the claims of the parties involved in the enquiry.

The identification of such discourses appears to be largely an intuitive and interpretative process. Although researchers often claim to have used coding procedures in their analysis, these are sometimes not described, and often no account is given of exactly how the analyses were performed. These are some of the common failings of discourse analytic research, and I shall spend more time on the problems with and criticisms of it later in this chapter.

An example of the analysis of discourses

In order to demonstrate this kind of discourse analysis, here is an example of an intuitive 'reading' of a small piece of text which I carried out myself. The material is a short newspaper article taken from the *Daily Mail*, January 1992:

SUMMIT VICTORY FOR MAJOR

John Major scored a victory even before he arrived in New York last night for the United Nations Summit. Weeks of careful diplomacy headed off a threat to Britain's place among the Big Five Nations. Germany and Japan both have ambitions for permanent seats on the Security Council but it was confirmed yesterday that the summit will not consider proposals for reform, which means the U.S., Russia, Britain, France and China remain the permanent members. Britain's swift success in pushing Boris Yeltsin and Russia into the old Soviet Union seat eliminated any need for reform.

Mr Major said: 'Why change a winning team? The priority is to determine the role of the United Nations in peacekeeping and peacemaking.'

Although this is only a very short piece of text, the analysis that I eventually produced was quite lengthy, and this is typical of discourse analysis. Quite small amounts of material can generate many hours of analytic work, and this makes discourse analysis a very time-consuming, labour-intensive activity.

The first step was to read the piece quite slowly and thoroughly, and to re-read it several times. During this reading, I was searching for recurrent themes, for coherent sets of statements or phrases which appear to talk about or represent events in similar ways, for metaphors that bring with them particular images of the events described, for words which seem loaded with meaning. This involved underlining words and phrases that seemed to paint a particular picture, and listing them on a sheet of paper so that I could scan them more easily for any sense of coherence. I looked for similarities and contrasts between them, asking myself what images and associations the metaphors imported, and whether there were any contradictions. An important question was also what images or ways of thinking about these events were being denied or repressed in these representations. Often the same word or phrase cropped up as a potential example of different themes or discourses. This is one sense in which discourse analysis is different from content analysis, where words or phrases may only occupy one coding category.

As a result of this analysis, I identified what appeared to me to be three 'ways of talking' that together contrived to construct the events of the story, which concern international relations, in a particular light. These might be termed 'international relations as war', 'international relations as sport' (and these two are closely related) and 'the personal and the impersonal'. Here are the lists that I made, and the intuitive reading that I subsequently produced:

'Battlefield/Conflict' terms:

Victory
Headed off (e.g. 'at the pass')
Threat
Pushing
Peacekeeping
Peacemaking

'Sport/Competitive' terms:

Victory
Scored
Headed off (e.g. 'heading' a ball)
Have ambitions
Swift success
Pushing
Winning team

'Personal/Impersonal' terms:

John Major scored a victory
Careful diplomacy headed off
Germany and Japan both have ambitions
It was confirmed
The summit will not consider
U.S., Russia, Britain, France and China remain the permanent members
Britain's swift success
Pushing Boris Yeltsin and Russia
Mr Major said

These terms were then used to suggest the operation of the following discourses:

1 International relations as war

The headline itself introduces this theme with the word 'victory', and it is followed up in the first line, which states that John Major 'scored a victory'. In the second line, the theme is reinforced with the statement that weeks of careful diplomacy 'headed off a threat'. The rest of the piece continues to operate within this general theme of conflict. The nations involved are seen as doing battle with each other, and as such there must be winners and losers. The physicality of combat is reflected in Britain's success in 'pushing Boris Yeltsin and Russia', and we are here further drawn into a vision of international relations as a battlefield where the combatants use physical force to respond to threats, and gain success and victory for themselves at the expense of their opponents. The final statement, giving the role of the United Nations as 'peacekeeping and peace-making', is a curious contrast to the war-like tenor of the rest of the article. The juxtaposition of 'battlefield' and 'peace' talk (and in that order) invites us to consider conflict as a valid route to peace.

2 International relations as sport

Closely allied to the 'war-like' theme outlined above is the image of the events as constituting some form of sporting encounter, a competitive game. Much of the terminology is borrowed from the 'battlefield' metaphor (or is it the other way around?), with descriptions of 'victory', 'swift success' and 'pushing'. But it acquires a particular game-like flavour when we read that victory was 'scored', that a threat was 'headed off' (this time, not 'headed off at the pass', but literally as a foot-baller would head a ball), that 'Britain's place among the Big Five Nations' is in danger (like a team's position at the top of a league table), and we are left in no doubt about the game metaphor from the final rhetorical question 'Why change a winning team?' Together, these images suggest that nations are like football teams, engaged in a competitive (though in the end not seriously conflictual – it is just a game) struggle against each other to achieve their ambitions, again necessarily producing winners and losers.

3 The personal and the impersonal

Most of the language used in this piece to describe the actions of the participants is impersonal and detached in tenor. Ambitions (usually thought of as pertaining to the personal hopes and aspirations of an individual) are here ascribed to nations (Germany and Japan). The non-specific 'summit' (seem-ingly independent of its human members) 'will not consider proposals for reform'. 'Britain' pushes 'Russia', as well as Boris Yeltsin, who, together with John/Mr Major is unusual in being personally recognised as an actor in the drama, and Britain addi-tionally enjoys 'swift success'. The heading off is done by 'weeks of careful diplomacy' (apparently without the interference of real people), 'it was confirmed yesterday' (apparently by no one), and the permanent 'members' (not referred to as, for example 'member states') are 'the U.S., Russia, Britain, France and China'. The language invites us to consider the events as somehow produced without the active participation of human beings with intentions, weaknesses, feelings, needs and so on.

The exceptions are the (very contrasting) victory of John Major and the ease with which Boris Yeltsin was pushed.

Having outlined these themes, an important next step would be to study their implications. What are the consequences of thinking of international relations as like a war or a football game (a war-game?), or as distanced from the concerns of real human beings? What effects on us does our identification with the protagonists in the story have? What recipes for personal and governmental action and for foreign policy are implicitly carried? In whose interests do these discourses operate, and whose do they marginalise?

As my aim here is simply to offer an illustrative example of the process of what I have referred to as 'the analysis of discourses', I will refrain from proceeding with this next stage of the analysis, and make some comments on the process. My 'reading' of this text has been subjective and intuitive, and was not produced by following a set of rules. Such an account, within the scientific paradigm of traditional psychology, would be deeply suspect, since it would be taken as purporting to reveal a truth, a truth supported only by one person's unsystematic and subjective interpretation. However, within a social constructionist framework my reading becomes one of many possible (and equally valid) readings of the text. Others reading this text may well have seen what they consider to be important themes which I have completely missed, and to regard as quite unimportant or even non-existent the ones I have described. The question becomes not how truthful this account is, but how useful it may be in understanding and perhaps eventually doing something about (in this case) international relations. It is important to note that, for social constructionism, the author of a piece of text and what may be thought of as his or her intentions are completely irrelevant to the analysis. In fact a key feature of poststructuralist writing is sometimes said to be the 'death of the author' – a piece of text may be thought of as a manifestation of prevailing discourses, and we should not be tempted to look inside the heads of particular individuals for their origins.

Before leaving this example behind, it is worth making again the point I raised earlier about the appropriateness of discourse analytic methods to the addressing of different research issues. One need not necessarily have to do a 'discourse analysis' in order to recognise that powerful images are being invoked in this piece of writing, to see how they are being used to particular ends and to grasp their implications. I do not therefore set out to defend the above as a suitable case for the analysis of discourses, and use the example only to illustrate something of the method.

There are at least two good reasons for not attempting such an analysis single-handed, as I have done here, especially where larger amounts of material are involved. On a pragmatic note, the analytic work proceeds faster if you do it as part of a team of two or three people. Themes that you have identified can be checked against each other's readings, and red herrings rejected. If two or three of you independently come up with similar themes, you can be more confident about the validity of your reading. While this has uncomfortable associations with the requirements of traditional scientific method (validity, replicability and so on), it is a recommendation which can also be seen as springing from what discourses are taken to be. Discourses are 'transindividual' (Parker, 1992). They are not located inside particular people, but exist in a linguistic community (a group of people), and 'bits' of them show up in texts of all kinds. Two or more people from the same linguistic community, by using processes of free association to evocative words and phrases, may be better placed to identify the discourses operating within a text than one person alone. Although it in no way pretends to be a recipe for 'how to analyse discourses', chapter 1 in Parker's (1992) book gives a number of (theoretically grounded) helpful hints about what to look for.

Some problems with 'the analysis of discourses'

The ultimate aim of the approach described above is to take a critical, progressive and political stance to the truth claims made by discourses which help maintain oppressive power relations, and to increase the 'voice' of marginalised discourses:

> Discourse analysts now can champion the cause of a particular discourse by elaborating the contrasting consequences of each discursive framework, and can promote an existing (perhaps subordinate) discourse (as the 'empowerment', 'giving people a voice' model of research). We can intervene directly in clarifying consequences of discursive frameworks with speakers (as in training or action research, for example),

as well as commenting on the discursive-political consequences of discursive clashes and frameworks.

(Parker and Burman, 1993: 170)

However, the basic theoretical foundations upon which deconstruction rests are relativism and the problematic nature of reality.
If there is no truth, only competing discourses, if all 'readings' are
equally valid, in what sense is one justified in saying 'Yes, but
some people are (really/in truth) oppressed'? How can one justify
privileging one discourse over another? This is a very difficult
issue for politically minded discourse analysts to deal with (e.g.
see Burman and Parker, 1993; Burman, 1990, 1991) and has made
it all the more important that the theoretical issues to do with the
relationship between discourse and reality get resolved.

Amongst other criticisms of discourse theory and research
generally (which I will return to later), and focussing particularly
upon Parker's (1992) list of features which, for him, identify
discourses, Abrams and Hogg (1990) put forward a particular
criticism of the political intentions of those in the discourse field.
They question the (implicit) assumption that discourse analysts
are especially well qualified to identify and help marginalised
groups. They point out that this would presumably mean that we
should try to give 'voice' to groups such as the National Front
just as much as to black people, women and gays, and question
the right of academics to make decisions about just which groups
ought to be empowered. It is fair to say that social constructionism as a theoretical approach seems to appeal particularly to
those holding broadly left-wing or liberal views, and the reasons
for this need to be examined, since there seems to be no particular
reason why right-wing views could not be equally well served by
social constructionism.

Potter also criticises Parker's view of reality, and the relationship between discourse and reality, on political grounds. He
suggests (Potter, personal communication) that Parker's view can
be regarded as just one version of the discourse–reality problem,
with its own political implications. As the status of his account is
not explicitly addressed by Parker, he may be criticised for doing
what other traditional psychologists before him have done, i.e.
representing their accounts as 'truth'.

Those who identify themselves as 'discourse psychologists'
and who have conducted research using 'discourse analysis' (e.g.

Litton and Potter, 1985; Potter and Halliday, 1990; McKinlay and Potter, 1987) have a rather different understanding of the term 'discourses' and prefer to use the term 'interpretative repertoires'. There are a number of reasons for this, which I will now set out (a clear account of them is provided in Potter *et al.*, 1990), before going on to describe the kind of work that is being done by researchers in this area.

Firstly, in recommending the identification and analysis of 'discourses', Parker appears to turn them into objects which have an existence independent of the people who use them and the contexts in which they are used. This approach makes the discourses themselves, and the relationships and conflicts between them, the focus of interest. Pieces of text, bits of interviews and 'natural' talk thus are only of interest to the extent that they yield 'clues' as to the discourses that are operating through them. Although Potter *et al.* recognise that such an analysis can be fruitful, they point out that this approach neglects what the speaker is doing with his or her talk, i.e. the constructive process in which the speaker is engaged, and of course the talk itself will vary according to the social context in which it takes place. Potter *et al.* believe it is a mistake to treat spoken or written texts as if they were (nothing more than) manifestations of discourses, and argue that to grasp the full power of a piece of text or talk it is necessary to understand in what political and interpersonal contexts the speaking (or writing) is being performed, to what purpose, and by what practical means this 'discourse' (i.e. the actual, spoken or written material) achieves its purpose.

A second, related, problem is that the identification of discourses has a tendency to become little more than the labelling of everyday 'common-sense' categories of events as 'discourses'. Parker himself says that in order to see a set of statements as somehow coherent and representing the same discourse, one has recourse to culturally available ideas as to what we think of as a 'topic' (Parker, 1990). Thus already existing ideas, objects, institutions, etc., such as the family, science, medicine, the individual and so on, each spawn an associated discourse. So we end up with 'familial discourse', 'science discourse' and so on, and we are therefore in danger of 'discovering' a discourse for every common-sense category we operate. This leaves researchers in a weak position if they want to question culturally available common-sense categories or hold them in abeyance until validated by analysis, because those categories are at the outset implicitly taken to be a valid part of identifying and describing the discourses that one wishes to study. Potter *et al.* give the example of 'the discourse of science'. This discourse is too easily 'mapped onto' the common-sense category or topic of 'science'. They quote a number of research studies (carried out within the 'discourse analysis' paradigm) which suggest that the social construction of 'science' is achieved not through the operation of a single discourse, but from the dual use by scientists of two different 'repertoires' (as Potter *et al.* prefer to call them); an 'empiricist' one and a 'contingent' one. By drawing upon the 'empiricist' repertoire, scientists were able to represent their personal theoretical preferences as deriving in a neutral way from 'the facts' as revealed by research. The 'contingent' repertoire was used to cast doubt upon the views of opponents by representing them as more influenced by non-scientific contingencies (such as political bias).

An additional problem with discourses as mapped onto common-sense topics is how one decides at what 'level', so to speak, discourses can be identified. For example, we may feel comfortable with the idea of there being a discourse of 'the family', a discourse of 'motherhood' and one of 'childhood', but could we further add to these discourses those of 'kinship', 'grandparenthood', and 'housework'? They are all recognisably 'topics', but exist at different levels of generality and specificity. Without some 'discourse-identifying' guidelines which lie outside of common sense, it is hard to see how we could avoid the proliferation of discourses until there were as many as words in a dictionary.

DISCOURSE ANALYSIS AND THE IDENTIFICATION OF INTERPRETATIVE REPERTOIRES

Within this approach, discourses are not entities existing in some independent realm, removed from the practices and discursive struggles of real speakers or writers. One cannot simply take, say, a bit of speech and directly apprehend the 'discourse' working within it, because what the person is doing with her or his speech will always 'get in the way of' its straightforward manifestation in that speech. Discourse analysts of the Potter *et al.* variety, then, begin their analytic enquiries not with the notion of abstract discourses of which their analysis identifies concrete examples, but with the concrete, contextualised performances of language from which they come to abstract, across many different examples, 'interpretative repertoires'.

Because of their emphasis upon the active construction of accounts, discourse analysts interested in the identification of interpretative repertoires (they sometimes also refer to themselves as 'discourse psychologists') very often use transcripts of interviews or 'natural' conversations as their material for analysis (e.g. McKinlay and Potter, 1987; Potter and Wetherell, 1989; Marshall and Raabe, 1993; Gill, 1993), although other kinds of material are occasionally used, such as newspaper reports (Edwards and Potter, 1992), television programmes (Potter *et al.*, 1991) and child-care manuals (Marshall, 1991).

I have already gone into some detail, in an earlier chapter, concerning what is meant by interpretative repertoires, with some examples of research. I will briefly recapitulate some of that earlier material here in order to demonstrate the rationale for the analytic approach. Interpretative repertoires (as the alternative term for 'discourses') are seen as linguistic resources or tool-kits available to speakers in the construction of their accounts. They are seen as analogous to the repertoire of moves of a ballet dancer: finite in number and available to all ballet dancers for the design of a variety of different dances suitable for a variety of different occasions. If you went to enough ballet performances, you would eventually begin to recognise the repertoire of moves that the dancers have available to them. The idea of a repertoire therefore also involves the idea of flexibility of use; the moves can be put together in different ways to suit the occasion (a feature not present in the idea of discourses as coherent, organised sets of statements.)

Researchers in the 'interpretative repertoires' field look for the metaphors, grammatical constructions, figures of speech and so on that people use in constructing their accounts. By examining the talk of different people when they are, say, interviewed about a topic, it is possible to monitor the way that some figures of speech, metaphors and so on keep turning up in the talk of different people. By abstracting such usages across different interviews on the same topic, it is claimed that the researcher can identify such repetitions of 'moves' as a repertoire. Therefore both variability and repetition are features which such analysts are looking for in their material. Variability can be expected within a single interview, because respondents can be expected to make use of different repertoires to suit their current purposes. Repetition across different interviews can be expected because the same repertoires will be used by different people.

Because they focus upon the way that people use language to construct accounts which have some 'warrant' in the world, discourse psychologists also look for the techniques by which people manage to justify themselves and their accounts, apportion blame, make excuses and so on. They appear to be using implicitly a model of the person as 'actor in a moral universe', and much of their analysis focusses upon how repertoires are used to create morally defensible positions for the speaker.

The process of analysis, in broad practical terms, appears to have much in common with that outlined with respect to 'the analysis of discourses'. Because they are frequently dealing with recorded speech, discourse psychologists must first transcribe their material, and have devised quite stringent methods for doing this in ways which are felt to convey the richness of the spoken word. Pauses, emphases, hesitations, overlaps and so on are all given visual representation. The transcribed material is then read and re-read closely many times, and a coding system is used to record extracts of speech. The coding categories at this stage are informed by the research question underlying the research.

Examples of discourse analysis

In an analysis of how the concept of 'community' was used in accounts of a riot in Bristol in 1980 (Potter and Reicher, 1987), as mentioned in an earlier chapter, the researchers initially extracted from the accounts all instances of use of the word 'community' and its synonyms. These instances were then analysed by looking at the words describing 'community' in each case. Potter and Reicher found that some descriptions were repeatedly used across different accounts. They then grouped these into four further categories, examples of which are shown below:

Friendly
Warm
Happy
Harmonious

Close-knit
Integrated
Tight

Grows
Evolves
Matures

Acts
Feels
Knows

These groups of terms represent the 'community' as embodying a particular, cohesive style of social relationship (e.g. 'harmonious'), as having an organic nature (it 'grows' and 'evolves'), and as having agency (it 'acts' and 'knows'). This 'community' repertoire was used by different people, who were giving quite different accounts of the riot, and achieving quite different accounting ends with their use of this repertoire. This particular research example is now widely quoted, and I believe that this is an indication of the general lack of good discourse analytic research in which the theory is put into practice.

A central concern of those interested in discourse analysis is the processes by which people in interaction negotiate (morally) tenable positions for themselves. How do people manage their talk in order to justify their actions, blame others, excuse themselves and so on? These kinds of activity are seen by discourse analysts as a central feature of what is often going on in interactions between people.

To demonstrate how one might take such an analytic approach to a piece of text, I have used as an example a brief extract from an interview which was part of a television documentary. The documentary, an episode of *Violent Lives* (transmitted by Channel 4 in Britain on 1 August 1991), featured a number of young men who were currently serving sentences in a young offender's institution. The piece of text I have analysed is a transcription of part of an interview between a prison officer and four of the inmates, Jason, Coops, Miffa, and Goldie:

Officer: Now I want you to tell me what you think their [the audience of the television programme] first impressions are.
Jason: Convicts.
Coops: Hooligans and lager louts.

Miffa: Immature trouble makers.

Officer: And are you?

Coops: No but they're going to think that cos we're in here.

Officer: What are you?

Coops: Someone who's made a mistake.

Goldie: Human beings.

This is a nice example because the young offenders are clearly being invited to offer justificatory accounts of themselves ('And are you?', 'What are you?'). In their relatively powerless position compared to the officer, the TV crew and the audience, one of the few power resources available to the young men is their accounting strategies. Faced with the knowledge (stated here by Jason, Coops and Miffa) that the most widely held impressions of them will be as 'Convicts', 'Hooligans and lager louts', and 'Immature trouble makers', what linguistic resources do they bring to bear on the situation?

They each in turn offer an alternative construction of themselves which attempts to overturn the condemnatory implications of the above descriptions. Coops' reply, 'No but they're going to think that cos we're in here' invites us to see them as victims of stereotyping and labelling. It challenges the idea that those who get sent to prison must necessarily bear some personality deficit or have some behavioural problem. But it also implies that sometimes people who do not deserve to go to prison get sent there anyway. It appears to say 'Just because we're in here doesn't mean we ought to be here.'

This opens up the possibility for Coops and Goldie together to take this a step further, in response to the question 'What are you?' Having laid the groundwork in his previous response, Coops says 'Someone who's made a mistake', and Goldie follows with 'Human beings.' Both of these responses work together to elaborate further on this account of themselves as just ordinary human beings like anyone else. After all, everyone makes mistakes, do they not? We are all human beings and should remind ourselves that none of us is infallible. We all err, but some of us get caught and sent to prison for our errors. This account renders their situation as almost randomly meted out, so similar to the rest of humanity are they as people. It invites us to look at them and say 'There but for the grace of God go I.'

As with my previous example of the analysis of discourses, a small piece of text can be seen to generate a great deal of analysis.

There is still the problem of how to deal with the validity of my 'reading', and, as I shall go on to discuss shortly, this is a difficult issue in discourse analytic research. Not only could another person's reading of this interview be very different from mine, we would both be guilty of implying that our readings were somehow more worthy of attention (more truthful) than what the offenders themselves might have had to say about what they were doing. This is why discourse analysts recommend that their readings are discussed with the original participants and their responses incorporated into the report (this is part of 'reflexivity', about which I will say more in a moment).

PROBLEMS WITH DISCOURSE ANALYSIS

I have probably been over-emphasising the theoretical and analytical differences between the approaches outlined above, and have done so in order to bring out some of the issues for discussion. For the remainder of this chapter, I shall use the term 'discourse analysis' to refer to all varieties so far described, and will look at some of the problems and criticisms relevant to them all.

For the purpose of organising a variety of problematic issues, I will group them under two broad headings, 'reflexivity' and 'identifying discourses or repertoires'.

Reflexivity

I have already discussed above how the relativism of discourse theory makes it difficult to justify adopting one particular 'reading' of an event or text rather than others. This is a problem that occurs because of the theory's own reflexivity, that is, the way that the theory is applied to itself and its own research practice (discourse analysis). A discourse analysis cannot therefore be taken to reveal a 'truth' lying within the text, and must acknowledge its own research findings as open to other, potentially equally valid, readings. Parker and Burman (1993) note that the problem of the status of the researcher's reading (i.e. subjective interpretation) of a text has not been resolved. As pointed out earlier, this is particularly a problem for researchers who wish to take a political stance, and indeed they criticise the tendency for discourse analysis as a method to be taken up and subsumed by traditional psychology, thereby probably losing its political, critical usefulness. The Potter and Wetherell (1987) version of discourse analysis is also criticised on the grounds that it frequently looks only to the internal workings of a piece of text and ignores its wider political implications. Parker and Burman also are aware that researchers are tempted to 'close' the text to alternative readings other than their own, and in this sense are drawn back into the realm of the traditional research criteria of validity, reliability and so on. Abrams and Hogg (1990), specifically criticising Parker's criteria for the identification of discourses (the source of these is unfortunately not quoted in their paper), argue that in stressing the way in which 'discourses are realised in texts' the role of the interpreter is obscured.

Reflexivity also refers to the equal status, within discourse analysis, of researchers and their respondents, as well as of the accounts offered by each. This means that discourse analysts must find a way of building into their research opportunities for participants to comment upon their own accounts and those of the researcher. Sherrard (1991) criticises discourse analysts for not always meeting this criterion in their research, and Parker and Burman (1993) are concerned that attempts to include participants more fully in the analysis may not in the end escape the problem of power relations between researcher and researched. They agree with Marks (1993), who, in her own research, found that despite efforts at reflexivity, the researcher's own 'reading' was the one that appeared to carry weight. Thus reflexivity may only bring the illusion of 'democratisation' of the research relationship, which is worse than what it strives to replace.

Sherrard (1991) also claims that discourse analysts generally fail to address the part played by their own contribution to the discourse when they are taking part in the interaction as interviewers. She points out that interviews, like conversations, are constructed out of the 'moves' of both participants, and yet discourse analysts typically fail to examine explicitly their role in the production of the discourse they are analysing. Figueroa and López (1991) also note a general problem with discourse analysts' lack of attention to the methodological processes by which their data were gathered. In general, if one wants to say something insightful about the way an account is constructed or the discourses apparently in operation in a text, the production of the account/text itself, its context, history, intended audience and so on must surely be included in the analysis.

Identifying discourses or repertoires

The discourses or repertoires that are identified in a piece of text will, to some extent at least, depend upon what kind of text is being analysed (interview transcript, textbook, transcript of conversation, newspaper article and so on). This poses the problem of whether, when one analyses very different kinds of text, differences in what is found are due to discrete discourses/repertoires at work in the texts, or due to the same discourses being manifested in different ways in the particular textual forms being analysed.

Sherrard (1991) makes a related point, particularly relevant to the analysis of the spoken word. She points out that speakers in a particular speech community, at a particular point in history, will have available to them a restricted range of ways of talking about a particular event or object known to them. Their choice of words, metaphors, ways of speaking and so on therefore may not have any intended rhetorical force, but may be simply 'the way one speaks' if one is a member of that particular society or group. Therefore when discourse analysts are identifying linguistic forms, which they then group together as part of repertoires which in turn are seen as producing a particular kind of account with a particular purpose, the real linguistic choices available to speakers must be considered. For example, Sherrard points out that to use the form of address 'Miss' rather than 'Ms' would be rhetorical (i.e. used for constructing an account of a person to represent her in a particular light) only if 'Ms' was truly available to the person as an alternative mode of address in his or her speech community, and one which he or she had therefore chosen to reject in fashioning his or her account. A person being interviewed in the 1950s, or indeed in many places in the English-speaking world today, would not have such a choice available.

Even when an analysis may have been completed satisfactorily, researchers often give only brief (or non-existent) descriptions of the processes they followed in compiling their report. While it is accepted that it is difficult to give more than broad guidelines as to how, in general terms, discourse analysis is performed, it should be possible for analysts to give quite detailed information about how, in their particular case, they proceeded with their analysis. In many cases, researchers offer no information about how the material was coded, or what criteria were used to identify bits of speech or text as similar or different. Illustrative extracts are commonly used to give the 'flavour' of the discourses/repertoires analysed, but readers, who do not have the full transcript or text in front of them, are not in a position to judge the status of the analyst's own reading. More rigour in the general reporting of the analytic process would also be of practical help to those wishing to attempt a discourse analysis for the first time.

ACKNOWLEDGEMENTS

The extract from *Violent Lives* is reproduced with permission. The programme was produced by Compass Films for Channel Four Television Company. I am here indebted to Caroline Clark for use of her transcribed material.

SUGGESTED FURTHER READING

Burman, E. and Parker, I. (eds) (1993) *Discourse Analytic Research: Repertoires and Readings of Texts in Action*, London: Routledge. A useful collection of readings based on research studies using discourse analysis. It includes a good chapter by the editors, outlining the many theoretical and methodological problems with the approach.
Hollway, W. (1989) *Subjectivity and Method in Psychology: Gender, Meaning and Science*, London: Sage. Using gender as her focus, Hollway takes a critical look at psychology, its methods and the assumptions underlying the model of science that it has adopted.

Glossary

Behaviourism. School of psychological theory which holds that the observation and description of overt behaviour are all that is needed to understand human beings.

Cognitivism. In this context, the assumption that psychological processes such as thinking, perception and reasoning find expression in individual and interpersonal behaviour.

Critical realism. See **realism**.

Deconstruction. The analysis of a piece of text to reveal the discourses and systems of oppositions operating within it.

Determinism. A style of thinking in which all human action or experience is assumed to be directly caused.

Discourse. This term is used primarily in two senses: (i) to refer to a systematic, coherent set of images, metaphors and so on that construct an object in a particular way, and (ii) to refer to the actual spoken interchanges between people.

Discourse analysis. The analysis of a piece of text in order to reveal either the discourses operating within it or the linguistic and rhetorical devices that are used in its construction.

Empiricism. The view that the only valid knowledge is that which is derived from observation and experiment.

Epistemology. The philosophy of knowledge; The study of the nature of knowledge and the methods of obtaining it.

Essentialism. The view that objects (including people) have an essential, inherent nature which can be discovered.

Humanism. Often used in the narrow sense of referring to the view of human beings as individual agents who are the originators of their own thoughts and actions.

Idealism. An ontological theory which states that only minds and their ideas exist. Material objects exist only as objects of perception. This is opposed to **realism**.

Interpretative repertoire. Term introduced by Potter and Wetherell (1987) to refer to a stock of culturally available linguistic devices from which people may construct accounts.

Ontology. The study of being and existence. The attempt to discover the fundamental categories of what exists.

Perspectivism. See **relativism**.

Positivism. The belief that we can only know what we can immediately apprehend. That which exists is what we perceive to exist.

Postmodernism. The rejection of 'grand narratives' in theory and the replacement of a search for truth with a celebration of the multiplicity of (equally valid) perspectives.

Poststructuralism. The rejection of structuralism's search for explanatory structures underlying social phenomena. In linguistics, also the view that the meanings of signs (eg. words) are not fixed, but shifting and contestible.

Realism. An ontological theory which states that the external world exists independently of being thought of or perceived. This is opposed to **idealism. Critical realism** is the view that, although we cannot be directly aware of the material objects in the world, nevertheless our perceptions do give us some kind of knowledge of them.

Reflexivity. Term used by social constructionists to refer to the application of the theory back onto itself and its practices.

Relativism. The view that there can be no ultimate truth, and that therefore all perspectives are equally valid.

Structuralism. The belief in and search for explanatory structures which are held to give rise to the 'surface' phenomena of, for example, society or human thought and behaviour.

Subjectivity. Term used by social constructionists to refer to the state of personhood or selfhood. It replaces traditional psychological terms such as 'personality' and 'individual'.

Text. Anything which can be 'read' for meaning. As well as written material, this potentially includes pictorial images, clothes, buildings, food, consumer goods and so on.

Bibliography

Abrams, D. and Hogg, M.A. (1990) 'The context of discourse: let's not throw the baby out with the bathwater', *Philosophical Psychology* 3 (2) 219–225.

Adorno, T., Frenkel-Brunswick, E., Levinson, D. and Sanford, R.N. (1950) *The Authoritarian Personality*, New York: Harper.

Allport, F. (1924) *Social Psychology*, Boston: Houghton Mifflin.

Althusser, L. (1971) *Lenin and Philosophy and Other Essays*, London: New Left Books.

Aries, P. (1962) *Centuries of Childhood: A Social History of Family Life*, New York: Vintage.

Armistead, N. (1974) *Reconstructing Social Psychology*, Harmondsworth: Penguin.

Arnot, M. and Weiner, G. (eds) (1987) *Gender and the Politics of Schooling* London: Hutchinson.

Asch, S. (1956) 'Studies of independence and conformity: a minority of one against a unanimous majority', *Psychological Monographs* 70: 9.

Ashmore, M. (1989) *The Reflexive Thesis*, Chicago: Chicago University Press.

Austin, J.L. (1962) *How to Do Things with Words*, London: Oxford University Press.

Averill, J. (1985) 'The social construction of emotion: with special reference to love', in K.J. Gergen and K.E. Davis (eds) *The Social Construction of the Person*, New York: Springer-Verlag.

Azjen, I. and Fishbein, M. (1980) *Understanding Attitudes and Predicting Social Behaviour*, Englewood Cliffs, NJ: Prentice-Hall.

Barnes, B. (1977) *Interests and the Growth of Knowledge*, London: Routledge and Kegan Paul.

Bateson, G. (1972) *Steps to an Ecology of Mind*, New York: Chandler.

Berger, P. and Luckmann, T. (1966) *The Social Construction of Reality: A Treatise in the Sociology of Knowledge*, New York: Doubleday and Co.

Billig, M. (1987) *Arguing and Thinking: A Rhetorical Approach to Social Psychology*, Cambridge: Cambridge University Press.

Billig, M. (1990) 'Rhetoric of social psychology', in I. Parker and J. Shotter (eds) *Deconstructing Social Psychology*, London: Routledge.

Billig, M. (1991) *Ideologies and Beliefs*, London: Sage.
Billig, M., Condor, S., Edwards, D., Gane, M., Middleton, D. and Radley, A. (1988) *Ideological Dilemmas: A Social Psychology of Everyday Thinking*, London: Sage.
Brown, P. (1973) *Radical Psychology*, London: Tavistock.
Burman, E. (1990) 'Differing with deconstruction: a feminist critique', in I. Parker and J. Shotter (eds) *Deconstructing Social Psychology*, London: Routledge.
Burman, E. (1991) 'What discourse is not', *Philosophical Psychology* 4 (3): 325–342.
Burman, E. and Parker, I. (eds) (1993) *Discourse Analytic Research: Repertoires and Readings of Texts in Action*, London: Routledge.
Burr, V. and Butt, T.W. (1993) 'Personal and social constructionism', unpublished paper, University of Huddersfield.
Bury, M.R. (1986) 'Social constructionism and the development of medical sociology', *Sociology of Health and Illness* 8 (2): 137–169.
Cattell, R.B. (1946) *Description and Measurement of Personality*, New York: Harcourt, Brace and World.
Cattell, R.B. and IPAT staff (1986) *The 16 Personality Factor Questionnaire*, Palo Alto, CA: IPAT.
Chodorow, N. (1978) *The Reproduction of Mothering*, Berkeley, CA: University of California Press.
Clegg, S.R. (1989) *Frameworks of Power*, London: Sage.
Craib, I. (1984) *Modern Social Theory: From Parsons to Habermas*, Brighton: Harvester Wheatsheaf.
Craib, I. (1992) *Anthony Giddens*, London: Routledge.
Davies, B. and Harré, R. (1990) 'Positioning: the discursive production of selves', *Journal for the Theory of Social Behaviour* 20 (1): 43–63.
Derrida, J. (1974) *Of Grammatology*, Baltimore, MD: Johns Hopkins University Press.
Derrida, J. (1978) *Writing and Difference*, Chicago: University of Chicago Press.
Derrida, J. (1981) *Dissemination*, Chicago: University of Chicago Press.
Edwards, D. and Potter, J. (1992) *Discursive Psychology*, London: Sage.
Edwards, D., Ashmore, M. and Potter, J. (forthcoming) 'Death and furniture: the rhetoric, politics and theory of bottom line arguments against relativism', *History of the Human Sciences*.
Eysenck, H.J. and Eysenck, S.B.G. (1967) *Personality Structure and Measurement*, London: Routledge and Kegan Paul.
Figueroa, H. and López, M. (1991) 'Commentary on Discourse Analysis Workshop/Conference', paper for Second Discourse Analysis Workshop/Conference, Manchester Polytechnic, July.
Fishbein, M. and Azjen, I. (1975) *Belief, Attitudes, Intention and Behaviour: An Introduction to Theory and Research*, Reading, MA: Addison-Wesley.
Foucault, M. (1972) *The Archaeology of Knowledge*, London: Tavistock.
Foucault, M. (1976) *The History of Sexuality: An Introduction*, Harmondsworth: Penguin.
Foucault, M. (1979) *Discipline and Punish*, Harmondsworth: Penguin.
Frisby, D. and Sayer, D. (1986) *Society*, Chichester: Ellis Horwood.

Fromm, E. (1942/1960) *The Fear of Freedom*, London: Routledge and Kegan Paul.

Fromm, E. (1955) *The Sane Society*, New York: Rinehart.

Frosh, S. (1987) *The Politics of Psychoanalysis: An Introduction to Freudian and Post-Freudian Theory*, London: Macmillan.

Gabbay, J. (1982) 'Asthma attacked?', in P. Wright and A. Treacher (eds) *The Problems of Medical Knowledge*, Edinburgh: Edinburgh University Press.

Gavey, N. (1989) 'Feminist poststructuralism and discourse analysis', *Psychology of Women Quarterly* 13: 459–475.

Gergen, K.J. (1973) 'Social psychology as history', *Journal of Personality and Social Psychology* 26: 309–320.

Gergen, K.J. (1985) 'The social constructionist movement in modern psychology', *American Psychologist* 40: 266–275.

Gergen, K.J. (1989) 'Warranting voice and the elaboration of the self', in J. Shotter and K.J. Gergen (eds) *Texts of Identity*, London: Sage.

Gergen, K.J. and Gergen, M.M. (1984) 'The social construction of narrative accounts', in K.J. Gergen and M.M. Gergen (eds) *Historical Social Psychology*, Hillsdale, NJ: Lawrence Erlbaum Associates.

Gergen, K.J. and Gergen, M.M. (1986) 'Narrative form and the construction of psychological science', in T.R. Sarbin (ed.) *Narrative Psychology: The Storied Nature of Human Conduct*, New York: Praeger.

Giddens, A. (1984) *The Constitution of Society: An Outline of the Theory of Structuralism*, Cambridge: Polity Press.

Gilbert, G.N. and Mulkay, M. (1984) *Opening Pandora's Box: A Sociological Analysis of Scientists' Discourse*, Cambridge: Cambridge University Press.

Gill, R. (1993) 'Justifying injustice: broadcasters' accounts of inequality in radio', in E. Burman and I. Parker (eds) *Discourse Analytic Research: Repertoires and Readings of Texts in Action*, London: Routledge.

Gilligan, C. (1982) *In a Different Voice: Psychological Theory and Women's Development*, Cambridge, MA: Harvard University Press.

Harré, R. (1983) *Personal Being: A Theory for Individual Psychology*, Oxford: Blackwell.

Harré, R. (1985) 'The language game of self-ascription: a note', in K.J. Gergen and K.E. Davis (eds) *The Social Construction of the Person*, New York: Springer-Verlag.

Harré, R. (ed.) (1986a) *The Social Construction of Emotions*, Oxford: Blackwell.

Harré, R. (1986b) 'The step to social constructionism', in M. Richards and P. Light (eds) *Children of Social Worlds*, Cambridge: Polity Press.

Harré, R. (1989) 'Language games and the texts of identity', in J. Shotter and K.J. Gergen (eds) *Texts of Identity*, London: Sage.

Harré, R. and Gillett, G. (1994) *The Discursive Mind*, London: Sage.

Harré, R. and Secord, P.F. (1972) *The Explanation of Social Behaviour*, Oxford: Blackwell.

Heider, F. and Simmel, E. (1944) 'A study of apparent behaviour', *American Journal of Psychology* 57: 243–259.

Henriques, J., Hollway, W., Urwin, C., Venn, C. and Walkerdine, V. (1984) *Changing the Subject: Psychology, Social Regulation and Subjectivity*, London: Methuen.

Hilgard, E.R., Atkinson, R.C. and Atkinson, R.L. (1971) *Introduction to Psychology*, fifth edition, New York: Harcourt Brace Jovanovich Inc.

Hollway, W. (1981) ' "I just wanted to kill a woman." Why? The Ripper and male sexuality', *Feminist Review* 9: 33–40.

Hollway, W. (1984) 'Gender difference and the production of subjectivity', in J. Henriques, W. Hollway, C. Urwin, C. Venn and V. Walkerdine (eds) *Changing the Subject: Psychology, Social Regulation and Subjectivity*, London: Methuen.

Hollway, W. (1989) *Subjectivity and Method in Psychology: Gender, Meaning and Science*, London: Sage.

Kelly, G. (1955) *The Psychology of Personal Constructs*, New York and London: W.W. Norton.

Kitzinger, C. (1987) *The Social Construction of Lesbianism*, London: Sage.

Kitzinger, C. (1989) 'The regulation of lesbian identities: liberal humanism as an ideology of social control', in J. Shotter and K.J. Gergen (eds) *Texts of Identity*, London: Sage.

Kitzinger, C. (1990) 'The rhetoric of pseudoscience', in I. Parker and J. Shotter (eds) *Deconstructing Social Psychology*, London and New York: Routledge.

Kitzinger, C. (1992) 'The individuated self-concept: a critical analysis of social constructionist writing on individualism', in G. Breakwell (ed.) *Social Psychology of Identity and the Self Concept*, London: Surrey University Press in association with Academic Press.

Laclau, E. (1983) 'The impossibility of society', *Canadian Journal of Political and Social Theory* 7: 21–24.

Lalljee, M. and Widdicombe, S. (1989) 'Discourse analysis', in A.M. Coleman and J.G. Beaumont (eds) *Psychology Survey 7*, London and Leicester: British Psychological Society and Routledge.

Latané, B. and Darley, J.M. (1970) *The Unresponsive Bystander: Why Doesn't He Help?*, New York: Appleton-Century-Crofts.

Litton, I. and Potter, J. (1985) 'Social representations in the ordinary explanation of a "riot" ', *European Journal of Social Psychology* 15: 371–388.

Lutz, C. (1982) 'The domain of emotion words on Ifaluk', *American Ethnologist* 9: 113–128.

Lutz, C. (1990) 'Morality, domination and understanding of "justifiable anger" among the Ifaluk', in G.R. Semin and K.J. Gergen (eds) *Everyday Understanding*, London: Sage.

MacDonnell, D. (1986) *Theories of Discourse: An Introduction*, Oxford: Blackwell.

McKinlay, A. and Potter, J. (1987) 'Model discourse: interpretative repertoires in scientists' conference talk', *Social Studies of Science* 17: 443–463.

Macnaghten, P. (1993) 'Discourses of nature: argumentation and power', in E. Burman and I. Parker (eds) *Discourse Analytic Research*, London and New York: Routledge.

Mancuso, J.C. (1986) 'The acquisition and use of narrative grammar structure', in T.R. Sarbin (ed.) *Narrative Psychology: The Storied Nature of Human Conduct*, New York: Praeger.

Marks, D. (1993) 'Case-conference analysis and action research', in E. Burman and I. Parker (eds) *Discourse Analytic Research: Repertoires and Readings of Texts in Action*, London: Routledge.

Marshall, H. (1991) 'The social construction of motherhood: an analysis of childcare and parenting manuals', in E. Lloyd, A. Phoenix and A. Woolett (eds) *Motherhood: Meanings, Practices and Ideologies*, London: Sage.

Marshall, H. and Raabe, B. (1993) 'Political discourse: talking about nationalization and privatization', in E. Burman and I. Parker (eds) *Discourse Analytic Research: Repertoires and Readings of Texts in Action*, London: Routledge.

Mead, G.H. (1934) *Mind, Self and Society*, Chicago: University of Chicago Press.

Michotte, A.E. (1963) *The Perception of Causality*, London: Methuen.

Mischel, W. (1968) *Personality and Assessment*, New York and London: Wiley.

Moscovici, S., Lage, S. and Naffrechoux, M. (1969) 'Influence of a consistent minority on the responses of a majority in a colour perception task', *Sociometry* 32: 365–380.

Mulkay, M. (1985) *The Word and the World: Explorations in the Form of Sociological Analysis*, London: Allen and Unwin.

Parker, I. (1990) 'Discourse: definitions and contradictions', *Philosophical Psychology* 3 (2) 189–204.

Parker, I. (1992) *Discourse Dynamics: Critical Analysis for Social and Individual Psychology*, London: Routledge.

Parker, I. and Burman, E. (1993) 'Against discursive imperialism, empiricism and construction: thirty two problems with discourse analysis', in E. Burman and I. Parker (eds) *Discourse Analytic Research: Repertoires and Readings of Texts in Action*, London: Routledge.

Parker, I. and Shotter, J. (eds) (1990) *Deconstructing Social Psychology*, London and New York: Routledge.

Piaget, J. (1952) *The Origins of Intelligence in Children*, New York: W.W. Norton.

Potter, J. and Collie, F. (1989) ' "Community care" as persuasive rhetoric: a study of discourse', *Disability, Handicap and Society* 4 (1) 57–64.

Potter, J. and Halliday, Q. (1990) 'Community leaders: a device for warranting versions of crowd events', *Journal of Pragmatics* 14: 225–241.

Potter, J. and Reicher, S. (1987) 'Discourses of community and conflict: the organisation of social categories in accounts of a "riot" ', *British Journal of Social Psychology* 26: 25–40.

Potter, J. and Wetherell, M. (1987) *Discourse and Social Psychology: Beyond Attitudes and Behaviour*, London: Sage.

Potter, J. and Wetherell, M. (1989) 'Fragmented ideologies: accounts of educational failure and positive discrimination', *Text* 9 (2): 175–190.

Potter, J., Wetherell, M. and Chitty, A. (1991) 'Quantification rhetoric – cancer on television', *Discourse and Society* 2(3): 333–365.

Potter, J., Wetherell, M., Gill, R. and Edwards, D. (1990) 'Discourse: noun, verb or social practice?', *Philosophical Psychology* 3 (2): 205–217.

Rosch, E.H. (1973) 'Natural categories', *Cognitive Psychology* 4: 328–350.

Rose, N. (1989) *Governing the Soul: The Shaping of the Private Self*, London: Routledge.

Rose, N. (1990) 'Psychology as a "social" science', in I. Parker and J. Shotter (eds) *Deconstructing Social Psychology*, London and New York: Routledge.

Sampson, E.E. (1989) 'The deconstruction of the self', in J. Shotter and K.J. Gergen (eds) *Texts of Identity*, London: Sage.

Sampson, E.E. (1990) 'Social psychology and social control', in I. Parker and J. Shotter (eds) *Deconstructing Social Psychology*, London: Routledge.

Sapir, E. (1947) *Selected Writings in Language, Culture and Personality*, Los Angeles: University of California Press.

Sarbin, T.R. (1986) 'The narrative as root metaphor for psychology', in T.R. Sarbin (ed.) *Narrative Psychology: The Storied Nature of Human Conduct*, New York: Praeger.

Sarup, M. (1988) *An Introductory Guide to Post-structuralism and Postmodernism*, Hemel Hempstead: Harvester Wheatsheaf.

Saussure, F. de (1974) *Course in General Linguistics*, London: Fontana.

Sawicki, J. (1991) *Disciplining Foucault: Feminism, Power and the Body*, London: Routledge.

Sherrard, C. (1991) 'Developing discourse analysis', *Journal of General Psychology* 118 (2): 171–179.

Shotter, J. (1993a) *Conversational Realities*, London: Sage.

Shotter, J. (1993b) *Cultural Politics of Everyday Life*, Buckingham: Open University Press.

Shotter, J. and Gergen, K.J. (eds) (1989) *Texts of Identity*, London: Sage.

Smith, J. (1981) 'Self and experience in Maori culture', in P. Heelas and A. Lock (eds) *Indigenous Psychologies*, London: Academic Press.

Squire, C. (1990) 'Crisis what crisis? Discourses and narratives of the "social" in social psychology', in I. Parker and J. Shotter (eds) *Deconstructing Social Psychology*, London: Routledge.

Stenner, P. (1993) 'Discoursing jealousy', in E. Burman and I. Parker (eds) *Discourse Analytic Research*, London and New York: Routledge.

Sutton-Smith, B. (1986) 'Children's fiction-making', in T.R. Sarbin (ed.) *Narrative Psychology: The Storied Nature of Human Conduct*, New York: Praeger.

Thompson, J.B. (1990) *Ideology and Modern Culture*, Cambridge: Polity Press.

Walkerdine, V. (1981) 'Sex, power and pedagogy', *Screen Education* 38: 14–23. Reprinted in M. Arnot and G. Weiner (eds) (1987) *Gender and the Politics of Schooling*, London: Hutchinson.

Walkerdine, V. (1984) 'Some day my prince will come', in A. McRobbie and M. Nava (eds) *Gender and Generation*, London: Macmillan.

Walkerdine, V. (1987) 'No laughing matter: girls' comics and the preparation for adolescent sexuality', in J.M. Broughton (ed.) *Critical Theories of Psychological Development*, New York: Plenum Press.

Weedon, C. (1987) *Feminist Practice and Poststructuralist Theory*, Oxford: Blackwell.

Wetherell, M. and Potter, J. (1988) 'Discourse analysis and the identification of interpretative repertoires', in C. Antaki (ed.) *Analysing Everyday Explanation: A Casebook of Methods*, London: Sage.

Wicker, A.W. (1969) 'Attitudes versus actions: the relationship of verbal and overt behavioural responses to attitude objects', *Journal of Social Issues* 25: 41–47.

Name index

Subject index